Praise For *Keep Sweet*

"*Keep Sweet* is filled with uplifting, thoughtful, easily digestible bits of good advice. Joshua Gonzales shares how he jump started his own life with kindness, positivity and a blazing streak of gay. YA readers will be eager to get their lives started after reading this enthusiastic road map."

—RICHIE JACKSON,
AUTHOR OF GAY LIKE ME: A FATHER WRITES TO HIS SON

"With honesty, self-awareness, and plenty of humor, Joshua Gonzales delivers a life-affirming memoir about seeing the beauty in painful experiences, standing strong against adversity, and staying positive no matter what life may throw our way."

—DANIEL ALEMAN,
AUTHOR OF INDIVISIBLE

"In his memoir *Keep Sweet*, Joshua has created a charming booster shot to the soul for young adults everywhere. He exudes an irrepressible optimism as he recounts tales of his life transition from an awkward Texas teen in a large Latine family to an out loud and proud, married gay actor working in New York City. But he also delivers the important messages of diversity, love, and inclusion that the world sorely needs right now. This book is a must read for all queerlings and those that love them!"

—BRITT EAST,
AUTHOR OF A GAY MAN'S GUIDE TO LIFE

KEEP SWEET

MY HOMEMADE RECIPE FOR A FULFILLING GAY LIFE

JOSHUA GONZALES

Cover and Interior Design: Damonza.com

Author Photo: Ambe J Photography

Joshwadam, LLC

New York, New York

KEEP SWEET: MY HOMEMADE RECIPE
FOR A FULFILLING GAY LIFE

ISBN 979-8-9869220-0-3 (ebook)

ISBN 979-8-9869220-1-0 (Paperback)

ISBN 979-8-9869220-2-7 (Hardcover)

Library of Congress Control Number: 2022916754

Subjects: Young Adult Nonfiction / Biography
& Autobiography / LGBTQ+

Printed in the United States of America

The information and advice contained in this book are based upon the research and the personal and professional experiences of the author. They are not intended as a substitute for consulting with a healthcare professional. The publisher and author are not responsible for any adverse effects or consequences resulting from the use of any of the suggestions, preparations, or procedures discussed in this book. All matters pertaining to your physical and mental health should be supervised by a healthcare professional.

This book is dedicated to all of those, who like myself, rarely see themselves in books. May this be at least one story for us, and may we build a future with countless more.

We are brave for living our stories. Heroes for sharing them.

INTRODUCTION

HELLO, LOVES! WELCOME to my first book! Thank you for joining me on this journey. Writing is incredibly hard and scary for me, but as a professional storyteller, I love to entertain, tell stories, and make people smile. First things first: I am not quite sure that I am—in any way, shape, or form—qualified to give "advice." Though how can I be sure when I've lived in a world that, for so long, tried to silence voices like mine? According to them, I'm too Latino, too gay, too poor, and too young to have anything important to say, but as goes my nature, I respectfully disagree.

I know there is a lot of advice out there from really awesome people who've objectively accomplished some great things (looking at you, Michelle Obama). My parents and I have come to terms with the fact that I'll never be Oprah, but I'd like to share what I have learned in my time on Earth as a member of multiple minority groups. And as someone who makes a living as a storyteller, I know that witnessing a few special life experiences from someone else can teach us multitudes about ourselves.

With that said, I am elated that you picked up this book or downloaded it from Amazon, because let's not pretend that anyone reads real books anymore. (I'm sure this is the line that got me rejected by every single publisher... Worth it? Probably not.) I can picture you reading this in a tiny font on your phone, sandwiched between two unknown men on the A train. One needs to learn about deodorant, one needs to learn about toothpaste, and both need to back up off you before you snap and shoulder-check them on your way out at your stop! Just me? Anyway....

One thing I *for sure* know is that my friends, family, and lots of folks on the Internet always ask me how I do things. How do I always seem so happy? How am I able to have a successful career in the arts, specifically as an actor? How am I able to build a happy life as a married gay man? First, I know I am incredibly fortunate to have these things. Or at least *feel* like I have these things. But I also know that I have worked very, very hard my entire life to get to where I am today. The most important thing I hope you take away from this book is that it hasn't always been easy for me, nor is it easy for anyone. I mean, growing up as a poor, gay, Latino in a very small, country town isn't exactly a silver-platter setup. Or, at least it wasn't for me.

The Internet was in its infancy, and social media didn't really exist, until I was in high school. I wasn't exposed to all the different kinds of people out there, nor was I easily able to find a community that I belonged to. God bless kids these days with their amazing, tolerant attitudes who use TikTok as a force for good. (Note: If TikTok is already over by the time you read this, please insert whatever social media app the kids are on in your timeline. Thanks!)

Growing up, I longed to see someone like me in the media, online, or even in a book. I searched for someone who shared my life experiences or anything I could relate to. Instead, all I found were Caucasian Abercrombie models, and absolutely none of them could ever be—GASP—gay! No offense to Texas, my family, or any of my childhood friends, but there was rarely anyone I could look up to. I fought a long, hard battle in my young adult years to become the person I needed as a kid. The person I dreamed would help me when I was completely lost. I made a vow very early on never to be defenseless, never to be completely reliant on someone else. If given the opportunity, I would turn around and help anyone like the person I used to be. Turns out, you have to create those opportunities for yourself because no one in this world wants to do that for you. Well, maybe they just don't have the time, ya know?

Now, I am definitely not THAT person yet. Sorry if you were expecting something different. However, I would like to believe I'm closer than I used to be. In some ways, I know that I am, but in most, I know I still have a big hill to climb. In case you didn't already know, improving yourself and becoming a force for good in the world is definitely not the easiest thing to do. But I know that I can help at least one person with my stories. If I can just make one person smile, or make one person's brain click with a realization that will change their outlook on life, then I know I did a great job.

One thing we all can count on is for life to throw us

curve balls when we least expect it. Some can be heartbreaking, some will be devastating, but most will be amazing. We have to keep ourselves ready to catch these curveballs. To see when one is heading our way and to make split-second decisions to perfectly intercept it before we get hit.

The best way I know how to stay in this state comes from the old improv adage "Yes, and." Or for my kweens, "Yas, and." This principle states that you never deny what is handed to you in the middle of an improv scene. Instead, you take what your scene partner gives you, and you build upon it in the best way that you can. If you walk into a scene, you have to be ready for your scene partner to be your brother, wife, or cat, and if they meow, then by-golly you pet them without hesitation and thank them for bringing you a dead bird. When you are prepared to go on life's crazy rides, whether they're good or bad, you are prepared to get the most out of life.

I know that, from the outside looking in, it may *seem* like I have had it pretty easy compared to others who are less fortunate. I've spent years building that avatar of myself for others to see because I strongly believe in conjuring up the life that you want. I, somewhat naively, believed that if I just started *pretending* I was where I wanted to be, maybe each day I would have to pretend a little less. Through sheer force of will, I could manifest the life I always wanted. Sure, I have had massive failures. I have bombed the big Broadway audition, my show has closed early, and I have feared that no one thinks I'm talented. But the people I love still love me, they are—for the most part—healthy, and I have a roof over my head and food on the table, so life is *chef's kiss* great!

Perspective is another one of my big wishes for everyone in the world. My generation (millennials) especially seems to struggle with this one. My peers, who have so much going for them, will still often only dwell on the negatives. They may not think they've had enough career advancement or may not have found "the one" yet, so they feel like total failures. Yet, when I listen to them complain, I always remind them that they are pursuing their dreams, they have food to eat, they have wonderful friends, and they are still in their TWENTIES (or thirties)! They always seem to feel much better after that. Perspective.

So thank you for picking up this book. Truly, it means the world to me. I promise you, if ever I see someone reading this out in the wild, I will spontaneously burst into tears. (I'm known to cry at seemingly simple but beautiful things.) I hope you have fun reading this. I hope I become your new best friend because there is nothing I love more than a new friend. (This trait is the bane of my extremely introverted husband's existence.) Most of all, though, I hope you are able to find something to take with you on your life's journey that will help you grow and push you to achieve a goal you've been putting off. Something that will help you realize you are not alone, and that though this life is hard, we can find good and wonderful little things that make it worth all the pain. And, even better, we can truly enjoy it! Because it would be a great shame not to, right?

We've been handed a glorious gift to make this life our own. To live how we want to live, to love who we want to love, and find meaning in our work that can bring positive change to this world for current and future generations.

While most of us work this magic on a smaller scale, it's not any less important. Keep in mind that it's within smaller circles that we are able to influence individuals. I wish that everyone fully buys into this mentality. Positivity, gratitude, and execution are the only things we need for a successful life. You will never be as rich, pretty, or well-connected as you want to be. But if you focus on you and put the best version of yourself out there as much as possible, you will be rewarded tenfold.

With that said, I'll start by doing the thing I love to do most: tell stories. Starting with movies, then video games, then plays, and now my own, I've always been incredibly fascinated with the power of stories. They completely transport us into different worlds, take us on journeys, and then return us exactly where we left, completely changed. Sometimes we come to know characters even better than we know our loved ones, or even ourselves. Is there anything else more magical or mysterious? Now I get to tell a few of mine. Thank you for choosing to spend some time with these crazy words that came out of my brain. It truly means the world to me. I will say that until you believe it because that is what is important to me.

KEEP ROOTING

Growing up as a tiny Latino boy, you'd think I'd have all these complexes about what I could do with my life or who I could become. That I was meant to live a smaller life. That I should barely graduate high school and get a job immediately to help my parents, foregoing college completely, and probably have one or two kids before I could legally drink. I was taught by the television shows and magazines of my day that certain things weren't meant for someone like me.

I always felt like I shouldn't want to end up at a top university or in a high position at a company, or that I shouldn't even expect to make over $30K a year. I didn't feel bad about it at the time; I just never saw people like me in those types of situations. And yet, somehow my mother and family instilled in me the conceited sense of privilege of a 6'2", Marvel-fit, mediocre white man in the 1950s. It's truly the mystery of the universe.

My father has eleven brothers and sisters, so I grew up very close to roughly thirty or forty people, most of whom were my cousins. If you aren't in-the-know, Latine cousins are more than just cousins. These thirty-plus people might as well have been extra siblings to me, a welcome addition to my two brothers. With the constant familial get-togethers, I was always in front of a crowd. Since the age of three, I reveled in entertaining them with a song, a joke, or a dance.

We didn't have much, and I knew that, but my family didn't always make it seem like a bad thing. It was just how it had always been. My parents definitely had more than they had when they were growing up, so we were doing okay. They had fought their way through high school, something I don't think their parents had completed, and from there, they found the best jobs they could: two full-time, salaried positions making far less than they deserved and less than many people around them.

My mother could've been the absolute fiercest stage mom in another life, easily rivaling Mama Rose. She always pushed all of her sons to be great—no—beyond great in anything that we pursued. She wouldn't accept anything less than a letter A grade. She wouldn't accept if her children weren't the best in the extracurricular du jour. She made us accept that we were going to go to college, come Hell or high water. (That is one of my favorite Southern phrases because it equally weighs the horrors of Hell with a light flood.)

While my mother's cutting criticism is infamous in our family, I guess it served her purpose well. She understood, though I don't think she quite realized, that we *could* have the very things that she had only dreamed of. Sure, there would be many people, mainly Caucasians, who would tell us those things weren't for us. But if we blended in, if we made friends with them, maybe we could beat them at their own game. Perhaps we could catch them off guard, resting on their laurels. If they thought we were "lazy Mexicans," then they wouldn't expect us to outwork them. Hard work wins every time.

My mother grew up very poor in a tiny, dusty town just on the Texas side of the border between Texas and Mexico. With the right breeze, I'm sure you could spit into the Rio Grande from her front door. I've heard legends of the outhouse, the single toy doll she had, and the one-and-a-half bedroom house that her five-person family shared. She married her high school sweetheart when she got pregnant, and they went on to have two more kids. But without college early on, no real education in the workplace, and of course, with the last name Gonzales, she never found a meaningful place in her working life.

Time and time again she found herself in lowly desk jobs, staring at old DOS computers or sorting through boxes and boxes of files. It was all unfulfilling clerical work that she despised, and—most insultingly of all—it didn't even pay well. I cannot even begin to imagine slaving away for forty years in a job I hated, only to have minimal fruits from my labor. It's enough to feel like a prison, and more than enough to make someone go insane. That dread and toxicity has a tendency to seep into all aspects of a person's life. I have no doubt it contributed to my parents' eventual divorce. If you aren't happy at the place you spend forty hours a week, it's even harder to be happy in other places.

I know my mother's grand ambition for life had pivoted from herself to her children, like many mothers. She would not let her children end up like this. She always made sure we knew to find a job that was meaningful to us. People like us probably wouldn't be paid well anyway, so why end up imprisoned behind a desk, the lowest rung on the ladder? She practically shoved me from the nest at seventeen, but then she was upset that she didn't see me anymore. Moms, am I right?

With her encouragement (read: THREATS), I gained the confidence that I could do anything in this world. Why *couldn't* I be in all the top classes in high school? Why *couldn't* I attend the expensive college? Why *couldn't* I move from a tiny Texas town to New York City to be an actor? The whole world was against me, sure, but the bleak picture that my mother painted seemed like the only alternative, so I would get there or die trying.

And I think, even to her surprise, it worked! My older brothers both have graduate degrees, wonderful families, amazing jobs, and are earning multiples of what our parents made. I'm not too far behind them either. I live in the greatest city in the world, pursue my artistic dreams, get paid to perform and work in the arts, and have an amazing husband, who is also, like, really hot!

While I've escaped the nine-to-five desk job, it still hasn't been a walk in the park. Life as an actor, or an artist, is hard enough, but then everyone else has a different view of what it means to be "successful." They apply their view of an actor's success with a slow side-eye or the over-asked question with *just* the right amount of condescension. They especially lay it on thick when they express disappointment that they haven't seen you on the obscure television show they watch. Listen up: only *we* get to define our success, which at least should be some measurable distance from our personal point A to our personal point B. For me, that doesn't include a graduate degree or working in an office, and that is okay!

Plus, my ethnicity has proven to be such a problem for other people in the entertainment industry that it is my own personal cry of rebellion to shine my heritage proudly every chance I get. That pride goes back to before I can remember. I know it started very young for me, when I realized that no other kid at school had such a big family or as many cousins as I had. I knew I had to hold onto my heritage in their world so as to not forget who I was. And of course, what did every Mexican/Tejano family hold onto in the nineties more tightly than SELENA QUINTANILLA-PÉREZ?

One of my favorite childhood memories, which is very recently now one of my *favorite* memories, is my fourth-grade book report and presentation. Mrs. Turner assigned everyone in the class to pick a celebrity, find a book about them in the library, and then write a report on their life that we'd present to the class. True to my little, baby gay, Latino heart, I picked none other than La Reina herself, Selena. Honestly, I have no idea why my parents were shocked I was gay because I might as well have been shouting it to them since I was nine.

If you don't know who Selena is, put this book down NOW and immediately go watch the 1997 Oscar-snubbed film titled *Selena*, starring the Oscar-snubbed actress Jennifer Lopez as Selena. Not only is this film required viewing for ALL, but it is a piece of visual literature that, in a Latine household, is only matched in reverence by the Holy Bible,

La Santa Biblia. Looking back, I do have some serious questions about my parents letting, nay, encouraging me to watch such a (SPOILER ALERT) tragic story over and over and over again, but man-oh-man I am so glad they did. Anytime we were at our cousins' house, that movie was on a loop.

Selena was a Mexican-American singer in the early nineties who was beloved by all. She came from a musical family (Los Dinos) that not only served as her band and back-up vocals, but also wrote all of her songs. Not only was she magnetic to watch and had amazing pipes, but she was revolutionizing the music scene at the time. Selena was able to cross over popular Latine music and popular American music seemingly at will.

My cousins and I knew all of her songs by heart and would sing them constantly, whether the movie was playing or not. We would grab whatever we could use as a microphone and all pretend we were her, a house full of Selenas. Performing for our imaginary fans, flying across the room in Selena's signature, salsa-like spinning. Elbows in, wrists limp, legs nearly closed, and SPIN!

Her songs began to play in both Mexican and American markets, joining the two, and paving the way for the future Shakira and even Jennifer Lopez herself. Selena was a feminist, gay icon before the world understood what those words meant, and before she truly got to rise to the height of her power, her time on this earth was tragically cut short.

The villain in this story is *hiss* Yolanda Saldívar *hiss*. Saldívar was an evil, crusty, devil-like woman-demon who infiltrated Selena's fan club. Selena—poor, little, innocent, sweet-baby-angel Selena—was too nice to Saldívar.

Eventually, Selena let Saldívar get close and manage the fan club and some of Selena's other ventures. Quickly though, it was discovered that Saldívar had been embezzling most of Selena's money. One day, when Selena went to confront Saldívar, a fight ensued, during which Saldívar pulled out a gun and shot Selena. Selena fled, bleeding out until she found help in a hotel lobby, but... it was too late. Selena died shortly after being rushed to the hospital. Troll-witch Saldívar locked herself in her car and threatened to take her own life while leading the police through an hours-long standoff. Soon the moldy-bread monster relented the weapon and let herself be taken into custody. Saldívar knows she is safer in her Texas prison, because if she is ever released, I'm sure Texans will enact their own form of justice upon her faster than her old, dry, crone throat could order a Honey Butter Chicken Biscuit.

This story became a legendary parable to the Latine population all over America. The notion that someone on the poorer end, the browner end, could rise to such stardom, fame, and accomplishment was the American dream for us all. Most importantly, Selena did it while celebrating who she was and championing her culture to people who were unfamiliar. I know I'll never *BE* Selena, but she helped me see that someone like me, from my background, could be successful following their dreams.

Since Selena never even got to reach her full potential, I've always felt this weird level of guilt. Whenever doubt creeps in, or whenever I'm nervous about the new next step in my life or career, a small part of me thinks, "Do it for

Selenas, anything for Selenas." Her bright light was shuttered before she had the chance to burst, so I'll be damned if I'm going to let her death be in vain by hiding who I am. I will lay out my goals and go at life full-force. Selena, Patron Saint of all Chicanos.

In this world, you'll always come across people who have a problem with who you are for various reasons. Not gonna lie, some are understandable, but most are stupid prejudices they were taught by ignorant people who want to keep whatever little power they have. It's shitty, it's unfair, and it's unavoidable. But rather than transfiguring yourself to fit whatever twisted slot they want to shove you into, it's more important than ever to double down on who you are, where you come from, and the value you bring.

Every day, I make a point to remember where I came from. Above all, I remember the looks, the snide remarks, and the disbelief when I told the people in my small hometown what I was going to do. Remember your haters. It's important not to dwell on them, of course, but remembering is great. They fuel me. They force me to make them eat their words and prove them wrong. A bully can't be a bully forever. Eventually, they'll either realize how wrong they were or end up needing you for something: money, inspiration, validation.

Take this particular college professor, for example, who antagonized me throughout my college career. Even though now he begs for donations, or begs that I give the university credit when I book a big job, he once exclaimed to me in his office, "Wow, you just have this big chip on your shoulder, don't you?!" YES! You're damn right I do! Because I've often had to outsmart, outwork, and outlast my peers time and time again to get to the same places. While I do enjoy it, it would be nice to not *have to* for once. But, I know it always makes me improve myself in the end. Practice doesn't make perfect. Perfect practice makes perfect, or at least gets you closer. I'll take my zenkai boost and use that extra power for my next steps.

Your roots are your foundation. When they run deep, strong, and are intertwined with others, you are unshakeable. And in the words of La Reina herself, "We got laughed at. My father was told that we would never make it. It's gradual, a growing process. It's not like it came overnight." Our roots should be important to us. Remembering where we come from helps us keep the perspective on what we have accomplished, and on what we can *still* accomplish.

KEEP GRATEFUL PART 1

TRUE STORY: ON my first day of kindergarten, my parents dropped me off, and I would not stop crying. All the teachers thought, of course, that I was missing my parents and didn't want to be with these strange people. They were wrong. I was missing my bubba. He had just gone off to college, and I hadn't quite adjusted yet. I swear I cried the entire day. Sorry to everyone involved, but *feelings*, man!

It's an old trope: little boys look up to their big brothers. Learn from them, idolize them, want to be them! I had two incredible big brothers growing up, even though we sometimes would smash each other's toys, or, the ultimate nerd revenge, delete each other's saved game data (OOF!). As the youngest, I was always the brat and often manipulated my parents into getting what I wanted. Sorry, not sorry. But I have since learned that my brothers are really cool. It was a realization I wish I'd had much sooner.

My eldest brother was The Chosen One. Unlike most kids who simply view their big brother as their hero, mine was a REAL hero. Like, for the entire country. AMERICA'S HERO. I'm not kidding. President Bill Clinton gave him all kinds of awards and stuff! Okay, let's back up so you'll understand.

It started suddenly one day when I was in the third grade. March 31st, 1999. I'll never forget that date. When I got home from school that day, it was just my mother and me in the house, since my other brother and father were at their weekly Boy Scout meeting. Oddly, we heard footsteps on our deck and then a solid knock on the door. We lived right off of a highway in the middle of the country and had few neighbors, but my mother figured it was a neighbor looking for her dog, or a kid peddling chocolate for a fundraiser. When she answered the door, there stood a parent's worst nightmare. A tall, clean-cut, all-American soldier in uniform filled the frame of the door. My eldest brother had joined the Army two years prior, a fact that my mother did not fully appreciate, as all mothers do, but never once did she think a day like this would come.

This stoic, yet gentle man greeted us very politely, proving that he himself must have been a Southerner. I remember his incredibly calm demeanor. He addressed my mom and asked if they could sit and talk about her son. I cannot even imagine what my mother's mind looked like in this instant. The only time you ever see a man in uniform at a soldier's family's house is when the soldier has died. It is one of the most bizarre ceremonial rituals we have in this country. I mean, I get it. But weird, guys. My mother quickly sent me to another room so they could talk. I think she hoped that I would go to my room out of earshot so that, if my brother had died, she could tell me herself. I didn't go to my room, though. I was too clever, even at that young age. My mother was too preoccupied to notice, so I snuck to our spare room, with the door slightly open, within clear earshot.

The man spoke to my mother serenely, yet matter-of-fact. He was void of emotion, so as not to tip the scales in either direction. He told my mother that my brother was MIA. Missing in Action. My brother had been on a patrol in a territory that was then known as Yugoslavia, and then he just wasn't. As of that morning, they had no idea where he was, but they were doing everything in their power to find him. "Missing? What do you mean 'missing?' How do you lose a soldier?" I remember my mother scolded, in the very feisty Latina way she often speaks, though this time dampened by the gravity of the situation.

I was still. So very still. I remember thinking I was in a dream or something. I wasn't sad or scared but confused. I was also a little excited. Though now I feel guilty about it, I imagined what kind of adventures my brother could be having. Did he set out on his own to defeat the enemy? Was he undercover and not even the Army could know? But I knew something wasn't right. The air was different. I could feel an iron weight over the household.

The man lingered until my father and other brother came home. He proceeded to go over everything with both my parents again, while I went over everything as best as I could with my brother in the spare room. My brother wasn't as excited as I had hoped he'd be when I told him the adventurous news. He was five years older than me, so he better understood that our brother was in danger. I remember him staring straight into my eyes, scared, and hugging me, and said it was going to be all right. That's when I felt the danger creep in. Though I knew my brother loved and cared for me, the actual display of affection was out of the ordinary, like it would be for most Texan boys. It wouldn't have happened if the situation weren't serious. My heart plunged.

I don't remember seeing my mother the rest of the night. I can only surmise that she was too distraught to think, let alone move. As my father tucked me in, I remember asking him if my eldest brother was okay. Another thing I feel guilty about. Making my father explain to me that my brother might not actually be okay, just about an hour after he found out himself.

My parents spent the rest of that night calling other family members with the devastating news. That night was the first time I ever heard my father cry. Full-on wailing, crying from the very pit of his being. It had woken me up in the middle of the night, unknown to anyone else. No child should have to hear a parent call out in agony like that. The sounds of their souls being ripped apart at the notion of losing their firstborn. I listened for a while and just waited to fall back asleep, not wanting to upset them anymore by being awake.

When the next morning finally came, I awoke to my parents telling me to come to watch the television. As I walked into the living room, half getting ready for school, I froze. There he was. My bubba! He was on the television! He looked a little different, a little bruised, but the title under his picture was his name: Steven M. Gonzales. He was on CNN. I couldn't believe it. He was okay! I think he was okay? Was he famous?

My parents explained that he had been captured, but thankfully, he was alive. The bad guys had him, but hopefully, he would be released and could come home. *Hopefully.* My ear caught that slip of a word, always too perceptive for my own good. "Hopefully" meant that it wasn't guaranteed. I finished getting ready for school, but my parents told me that I didn't have to go. They asked if I was sure I wanted to go. I said, "Of course." I loved learning. My friends were there. And there was going to be an Easter celebration with Mrs. Horner, so we might get treats!

At school, everything was fine… at first. My day was a little weird as a third grader. I started off in my normal class, and then after an hour, two other students, my best friends in the class, and I would be pulled out to go to our gifted and talented program for a couple of hours. This day, during our walk, I let out my secret to my friends. Abbey and John were stunned. They couldn't believe it and were sympathetic to the scary situation. They were a good squad.

When we arrived at the gifted and talented class, Mrs. Horner started the day by asking if anyone had seen the recent news about the three American soldiers that had been captured. The new POWs. Prisoners of War. Since they were the first captured American soldiers in a decade, it was the biggest news of the year. Every news station was covering the story. Most of the kids in the class started to chime in. So, I decided I should, too. I quickly told the class that one of them was my brother.

The rest is a blur. As soon as I said the words, I felt the world change. Mrs. Horner had a disbelieving smile and started to ask me why I thought that one was my brother.

And then the kids unleashed their wrath, as little kids do. "Nice April Fools' joke!" "He's making it up for April Fools!" It was, indeed, April 1st. The day after my brother had been captured, and the day I was telling my class, was April 1st... I lost it. I had always been a perfect kid and student. Never talked out of turn or raised my voice, but I lost it. I was a little kid being told I was lying about my hero being kidnapped and possibly killed by bad guys. All the pent-up fear and frustration is more than I would wish on any kid. Half blacked-out, I remember shrieking with every fiber of my being, desperate for them to believe me. Tears flooded my face. Mrs. Horner, who must have quickly realized the situation, ran and grabbed me to take me to be alone. All I remember is a couple of blurry images through tears: the classroom, my screaming, and flailing every limb with as much force as I could. I know Mrs. Horner had some bruises after. Knowing I would never act this way, she knew that this was the truth. She sat me down in the hall outside of the classroom and yelled to another teacher to go get the school counselor. God bless her, she stayed with me, trying to comfort me until the counselor came and picked me up to psycho/shrink me back to a passive—well, passive enough—state. Next thing I knew, my dad was there to take me home. I was so traumatized from the event, I don't think I said a word until I got home. April 1st is still a very sensitive day for me. I usually go ahead and tell friends and coworkers that it's a sensitive day and to leave me out of any plans they may have. And I still think about that event every year.

When we got home, I realized even more how big Steven's ordeal was. When my dad pulled into our driveway, our car was bombarded with about a dozen paparazzi. My dad pulled me out and tried to shield me as he pushed through the flashing lights. I couldn't see a thing. It was all so bright until we got through the front door. Luckily, our neighbor worked for the sheriff's office, so a quick phone call from my dad, and the press were relegated to the very end of the serpentine driveway to our neighborhood. However, the damage was done. My parents informed me that I could no longer play outside until further notice. I was devastated. I was a little boy. Our house was surrounded by a field, and rocks, and a forest that I loved to explore for hours. The nineties, am I right? At that moment, I developed such a strong hate for the paparazzi and press industries. I can never forgive them for ruining my outside playtime. No way!

All they cared about was getting a story. Oftentimes, their errors were so egregious that I was labeled as my brother's older sister, or my mother ended up being his wife. The reporters didn't care, and they didn't care that all the attention kept me a prisoner in my own home for weeks. I didn't return to school for the rest of the year. Somehow, the school system was nice enough to excuse my absence and grant me entrance to the fourth grade the next year. Good looking out, Scott Johnson Elementary!

Over the next month, things moved so quickly. About two weeks in, the Red Cross was able to see the three American soldiers. They gave them a couple American treats and were able to get letters from them. I remember being so excited, jumping on my parents' bed, as my whole family gathered around to read the letter that Steven had written to us. He included special notes to each of us and was sure to only include the good things. He was fine, physically, was being fed something at least, and was getting a lot of sleep in his cell. He had convinced some guards to play cards with him, so that passed the time okay enough.

Just to really hammer home how obnoxiously humble and amazing Steven is, and especially highlighting how selfless and empathetic he is to anyone that he comes across in his life, this is what he had to say during a midpoint interview he did with Reverend Jesse Jackson… Keep in mind, he was still in prison, and the future was still uncertain. Reverend Jesse Jackson asked him what message he had for his parents and let him know he would transmit the message back to them.

My brother looked at Reverend Jesse Jackson, then smiled brightly, looked down at his feet humbly, and this bitch said, "I hope it's all over soon. I miss you, Mom and Dad. I'm sorry you have to go through so much agony, and I hope to see you soon. I love you." And because he knew my mother would never let her child leave the table without consuming seconds or thirds he added, "I'm eating three meals a day, including bread with every meal. And I have a bed to sleep in. I'm even doing push-ups, and I'm getting to walk around." He had been through so much, and yet all he cared about was easing the fears of my mother, my father, my brother, and me. That is a level of selflessness that very few on this earth will ever reach.

After that brief hope, things kind of went stale again. Government people flew in and out of our house to keep us updated and cared for. My parents got a cellphone, a new computer with Internet access, and an email account. This was before everyone's toothbrush had WiFi, so it was a huge deal. They had everything they needed to be reached or to reach out and get the latest news. Different family members came to show their support and spent time babysitting us while my parents did interviews. They took care of all the household chores so my parents didn't have to. Not like they could focus on any of that.

Another two weeks passed. By then, Huntsville, our small Texas town, was plastered in yellow ribbons. The calling cards of support for POWs. This was the biggest thing to hit Huntsville since its founding! Everyone in town knew my entire family and jumped to our support. I felt famous. It was kind of cool, and made me forget that my brother could die at any second, ya know? Whatever works, right? Perhaps this was my first taste of fame that I would latch on to and chase for the rest of my life. The yellow ribbons were on every car, tree, and streetlight. People were wearing them everywhere.

Then one day, an official government person came to speak to my parents. I remember being told to sit, but I could stay in the room because—supposedly—it was going to be good news. President Bill Clinton was sending over Reverend Jesse Jackson for a second time to negotiate with the bad guys. This was before any, uh, controversy with the two of them, and they were both revered with immense respect. Especially Jackson. He went over there and met with the leader of the bad guys, and we held our breath, the only thing we could do in the now thirty-day-long nightmare. I didn't have any idea why they took my brother, what they wanted, or what their plans even were. I just hoped they would let him go.

Finally, the miracle came. We got the word! All the agency people who had swirled around my house for the past month took my parents away. I really had no idea what was going on, except that I was being watched by my aunt and uncle, and my cousins came over to hang out. Turns out Reverend Jesse Jackson had succeeded. He had managed to sweet-talk the three POWs to freedom.

Once released and able to speak with the officials, my brother got to make a phone call to my parents. For the first time in a very long time, they got to hear his voice, hear that he was okay, hear that the nightmare would soon be over, hear that their firstborn baby would be returned to them. Breathe.

My parents were quickly flown to Germany to pick up my brother. Neither one of my parents had ever been on an airplane, let alone a transatlantic flight to a foreign country. When they arrived, my brother had made it to the American fort in Frankfurt. The medical team had examined them to make sure they were all okay. My brother fared the best of the three, because of course he did. He is The Chosen One, and my big brother, after all. He escaped with only minor cuts and a couple of big bruises. One solider had a broken nose, the other had a couple of cracked ribs, but they all made it, and that's all that mattered. Grateful.

My brother was awarded two Purple Hearts and these special spurs for his service to the country through the ordeal. When asked what he wanted as a first real meal outside of the prison where he'd been kept, he responded: chips and salsa. He never bled more Tejano blood than in that moment.

I'll never forget when I saw him. We had gone to my

aunt's house in Houston to await the plane's return because there was no real airport in tiny Huntsville. When he walked in the door, I was so happy! There he was, safe and sound, the hero returned home after the perilous journey. I was so thankful I could be with him again. You have to realize that my brother was and is my favorite person ever.

Once home, my brother did have some adjusting time. Time to resettle, make sure he could be normal once again. He lucked out. He will rarely talk about how much adjusting he needed, but he seemed fine from the beginning. He definitely didn't have a hard time getting back into normal life, and it wasn't long before we were all hanging out and playing around like we always did. Another wave of gratitude washed over us, since oftentimes the aftershocks can be even worse than the traumatic event.

I'll forever be thankful that this chapter ended this way. I've gotten to grow up with my brother. I've watched him have a loving marriage to an absolute gem of a woman. He's a fatherly role model that I look to. He cut his teeth with me and is now raising two of his own, the first of which made me an uncle! I have learned the enormous amount of space we should keep for gratitude in our lives, as it is a miracle we are still here.

KEEP GRATEFUL PART II

AFTER A FEW weeks of getting reacclimated to civilian life, the REAL adventure began! Well, for me anyway. I'm sure Steven had already had more than enough excitement for a while and needed a rest. However, with America's obsession with war media, every single news outlet wanted an interview with my brother. The Army was a little selective, though, and wouldn't allow him on some shows due to some nonsense over disclosing military procedures, but he had other phone interviews, in-person interviews, and one reporter even traveled all the way to our small mobile home in Huntsville to interview him for *Time* magazine. An interview that I got to witness LIVE!

My brother was a capital-C Celebrity, and all of America wanted to show their appreciation for all that he had endured in the name of our country. My family was swept away to huge parades in Chicago, Palestine (his Texas hometown), El Paso, and even our very own Huntsville had a parade for us. Of course, my brother was the grand marshal of them all. He usually rode on a float or in an amazing Rolls-Royce, and I rode in the car in front or behind with my other family members. It was amazing to see all of these people showering him with support along the routes. I'll always believe people would rather support each other than hate each other because of this time in my life. Even though that has gotten much harder to believe lately.

In the whirlwind of all these parades, the biggest of them all was—GASP—Disneyland! YES, Mickey Fucking Mouse himself called and said, "Steven! Get your ass to California!" Being "lower class," we had never been to Disneyland or Disney World. I seriously thought it was one of those places I would just never see. But now we were actually going!

The only caveat was that we'd have to take an airplane to California. I had never been on a plane before, and I was terrified. This terror was only worsened by my brother, Andrew, who—in true big brother fashion—would regale me with stories of horrific plane crashes just so he could see the fright on my face and watch me go cry to my parents. My parents tried to calm me down and let me know that everything would be fine, but they annoyingly insisted that, no, we could not drive to California. Now, as a grown-up who has driven from New York City to Texas multiple times, I would like an explanation from them on this matter.

My only saving grace was that Steven would also be on the plane. Again, he had just gotten back from being a POW, so in my small child brain, he could probably fly the plane himself in some emergency if needed. Also, how could I turn down a trip to Disneyland? So, I mustered all the courage I had, boarded the plane, and didn't look back. And, I'll let you know that I only cried ONCE when we hit a little bump of turbulence before landing and the plane turned slightly to the left.

As soon as we landed, my family was greeted by some secret-agent-looking-type people, who immediately gathered us up with a firm, "We need to move now, or we'll be late. All of your luggage will be at the hotel for you." And folks, when someone starts treating you like a fancy celebrity, go with it! You may never have that opportunity again, so I implore you to relish it at any chance. I was lost in the hustle and bustle, thinking I was the shit, but they were really rushing us around for some reason. Why were we in such a hurry in the middle of the night?

Well, unbeknownst to me, we were heading to a release screening of STAR WARS: EPISODE ONE - THE PHANTOM MENACE. *Star Wars* was everything to my brothers and me, especially Steven. Like any good kid of the eighties, *Star Wars* was his one true fandom. We actually still have a tradition where we all go to see the newest film together with his kids, and it's one of my favorite things in the world.

That night, we would see one of the first screenings on release day of one of the most anticipated films of all time! As we walked up to the movie theater's entrance, we walked by a mile-long line of people camped out with sleeping bags and folding chairs waiting to get in. We shyly trotted by, hoping we were invisible to them, with an apologetic look meaning to say, "Yeah, I know you've been wearing a diaper for twenty-four hours, but like, I'm with this guy, and he's an American hero so,...sorry..."

Inside the theater was absolutely bonkers. There were people dressed up as every main character entertaining the packed crowd as we waited for the film to start. Leia, Chewie, Luke, Vader, and even C-3PO were there. It was a nerd's DREAM. It was MY dream! At one point, there were even huge beach balls flying around the crowd to keep us entertained. Then one guy deflated one and stuck his limbs through, climbed on top of a railing, and shouted, "I'm a beach ball, catch me!" then jumped onto some of his friends. Then that man had to leave, and the beach balls stopped, but luckily, the movie started right after.

Even though we had just flown in from Texas and it was a late-night showing, I didn't care! I stayed up the entire movie, staring in awe, and living my very best nerdy life until three in the morning, when my brothers and I finally filed into the hotel suite where we were being put up, recounting all of the coolest explosions and fights in that film. My brothers and I made pillow lightsabers and fought each other until we all got knocked out. The next morning, we'd wake up and head to the park. Our first day in Disneyland.

I had only heard of this mythical kid paradise, never thinking I would actually get to go one day. I was a huge Disney fan, but the only things I knew of Disneyland I had learned from the two-part episode arc on *Full House* where the Tanner family all go to Disney World for vacation.

Michelle, being Michelle, wins some Aladdin contest from the get. She is dubbed "Princess for the Day" and is granted three wishes from the Genie. For her first wish, Michelle wishes that she and her sisters can skip all the long lines and ride the rides at will. A smart use of a wish, as the lines at the park are always a bit of a bummer. Sounds absolutely bonkers, right?!

Now, if you have ever been to a Disney theme park, what I'm about to describe to you is going to be infuriating. I mean, you are going to rage out and go berserk, so I'd advise just skipping to the last paragraph of this chapter now. I know this because it has ruined all theme parks for me.

Upon entering the park, we were greeted by a team of guides. These were our own personal guides that would stick with us through the duration of our time. Not only were they there to make sure we hit all the best spots, but they would also help us do whatever we wanted. If we needed to eat, they would make it happen; if we wanted to stay and ride a certain ride multiple times instead of moving on with the itinerary, we could! But the greatest superpower of all was the legendary line-skip.

Somewhere out there, there is a top echelon of Disney cast members who have the superpower of line skipping. As we'd walk up to a ride, our guide would lead, taking us past the line, past the FastPass line, and right up to the ride car entry point. The guide would discreetly exchange a few words with the cast member operating the ride onboarding, and magically, we would be placed on the next available car. It was something people can only dream of, to wield so much power. Too much power...

In full Michelle Tanner power corruption mode, there were times when I didn't even have to get out of the car after the ride. I'd simply tell my guide that I wanted to go again, and as we'd pull up, she would relay that to the ride operator. We'd stay put on our car and go through the entire ride again. The look on the faces of those poor people who'd been waiting for an hour in line, just to see some little kid get his own private Disney experience. I'd like to say I felt sorry for them, which I do now, but I know my punk-ass, eight-year-old self felt like a Kardashian and gave them a half-wave and a barely audible, "Bye bitches!" I apologize to EVERYONE!

Since then, I've been to Disney World twice, and let me tell you, it is not the same. Even if your type-A husband meticulously maps out the itinerary, and zip-zap-zops his way through a FastPass schedule, you still have to wait a long time, and can never go on a ride more than once without devoting your entire day to it. I know I was incredibly spoiled, but if only I had known what it all meant! I wanna go back! I wanna be a baby!

Our final day at Disneyland as a family was the big event. Disney was hosting a full out, no marking, park parade with my brother and the other two POWs as the grand marshals. I stood with my family near the end of the route, a front-row seat to the spectacular. Tons of flamboyant dancers, intricate floats, and all my favorite characters passed by, stopping to greet and hug us. Then, finally, at the end, there was this gigantic red, white, and blue float. And perched atop this enormous vehicle were the three American heroes. As they passed by us in the center square of the park, confetti cannons went off everywhere and rained down a beautiful display of appreciation. I sure hope that they got approval from all three of them before releasing the confetti cannons, because now all I can think about is the horror of accidentally triggering post-traumatic stress disorder in a soldier in a huge public display. And of course, this was before we as a society had a huge handle on anything mental health-related, so I'm almost certain no one even thought of that.

Thankfully though, all the boys were all right. The Disney parade was a final celebration in their welcome home tour. A closing of a chapter in this highly unlikely story of three good soldiers becoming three national heroes. Safely home, retired from the dangerous work they had been doing, and off to start their own new stories.

As for me, I confidently stepped onto another airplane to head back to Texas. After flying the first time, I've never been afraid again. I just accepted it as a necessity if I was going to travel the world on the big adventures I began to dream that I would take one day. I would start fourth grade the next year, and everyone at school would know who I was. A weird feeling, but one that I definitely didn't hate. This would carry on throughout high school until I left for college. People would even stop my father and me at the local Walmart to ask how Steven was doing and where he was now. Seemingly every time we went. They would leave us with huge smiles after we told them the wonderful things he'd been up to since his time as a POW.

Because of this incredible adventure, I learned that the world is incredibly small. Celebrities, presidents, heroes, and the like are all just people, too, and we are a lot closer to them than most of us probably think. I got to see that seemingly simple people from tiny towns and humble beginnings can go on to achieve outstanding recognition for their contributions to their work, nation, and humanity. Unlike me, my brother is much too humble to ever admit that he did anything other than his job. He'd say that he isn't extraordinary, or a superman, but luckily, those of us who see him for who he really is, know that he is just that. He is one of the most hardworking, dedicated, virtuous, loyal, and honest people the world has ever known. Every day, I strive to be more like him, and I hope that you now do, too. We all could use a healthy dose of humility, and that "just doing my job to my absolute best" attitude. For bubba, I'll always be grateful.

KEEP OPEN

As PREVIOUSLY STATED in the introduction of this book, I am an actor, or a theatrical artiste, if you will. I'm not a household name that actually makes great money, but one that only a select few have heard of. I like to think that I'm just, like, really exclusive in that way. Yet, even without having made the jump to become a huge Hollywood success, I have been fortunate enough to work consistently and make a good amount of my income from performing.

Yes, this type of actor does exist, and we are all over New York City trying to catch our big break to one day become a household name. Or at least book a guest-starring role on whatever *Law & Order* we are on nowadays. I'm just kidding. I know exactly what *Law & Order* we are on. As a New Yorker and true crime lover, it is my life's duty to watch every single episode of *SVU*, and watch that badass lady-detective-now-captain take down those scary crime people, played by my friends! Go Team Benson!

Some people think what I do for a living is cool, and some

people look down on me, but my favorite people are those that gush over how they *wish* they could be so brave to follow their dreams! It's always a friend of a friend or a spouse of a family member. They prod with such fantastically researched questions, like "What is it like?" "What have I seen you in?" "So, you can make money doing that?" And then, after I've satisfied their curiosity, they always end with "You are so brave." "It must be amazing to just be following your dreams like that." And, my personal nightmare, "I could never do something like that." WHAT? YES, YOU CAN! Do it! You can be "so brave!" Yeah, it's hard and doesn't pay much most of the time, but it's absolutely worth it every time!

Since I am the youngest of three boys, I was pretty much the center of attention my whole life, and I demanded it stayed that way, much to my brothers' discontent. While I was always good at school, I quickly discovered that I could make friends by being funny and highly energetic. What better way to get out of being bullied than by making the bully laugh? My classmates enjoyed my shenanigans, and I had fun being disciplined by my teachers while they themselves were struggling to not smile. Every single report card said the exact same thing: "Joshua is doing very well in class, but he talks too much." Well, look who's STILL TALKING NOW, Mrs. WILSON!

Though I probably should've realized that the theatre was the place for me in school, it wasn't until one fateful day in seventh grade, when I saw my first live musical, that I made the connection. Growing up in the *peak* Disney years, I'd seen many a movie musical thanks to the incredible renaissance brought on by the one and only Alan Menken, the godfather of Disney. This man wrote the music to all of your faves: *The Little Mermaid, Aladdin, Beauty and the Beast*, and he achieved EGOT status doing so.

That's right, he racked up all of the awards! Emmy, Grammy, Oscar, and Tony! And with just one more Tony win, he'll even EGOT TWICE OVER! I swear all theatre folk owe him a lot more than anyone will ever give him credit for. Because of him, animated characters were my imaginary friends, and all of the lyrics to every single song have been locked in my brain since I was three. It did take a little longer, though, for me to encounter the theatre bug. Once bitten, I would be hooked for the rest of my days.

That legendary day was the day I saw THE Haley Phillips play Dolly Levi in the Huntsville High School production of *Hello, Dolly!* Fun fact: Huntsville is home to five federal prisons and death row in Texas. That's right, folks. If you are on death row in Texas, they will send you down to Huntsville, and you will be executed across the street from the church I attended growing up. CRAZY!

On this particular day, the entire seventh grade class won a field trip excursion to the high school. I believe it was some sort of reward for my class having better attendance than the eighth grade class for the entire year, or something like that, but who remembers the silly stuff? Side note: whoever decided that the "reward" for anything would be getting to sit through an old classical musical put on by a bunch of country teenagers deserves to be fired. Except maybe not, because I absolutely loved it, and it completely changed the course of my life for the better, so… IDK, I guess it's a toss-up. Anyway, this high school production of *Hello, Dolly!* was my first time to ever experience a real live musical. I'm fairly certain it was the first time for most of the cast as well...

All of us seventh graders were bussed to the other side of town to go to the only high school in Huntsville, and the only one within a hundred-mile radius. The auditorium was huge. It was probably the biggest indoor space I had ever been to up to that time. Our entire class fit, so it must have been about five hundred seats, all facing a cavernous stage sparsely decorated with shoddy wooden platforms. When the lights dimmed on the closed curtain, I think I expected a movie to be projected onto it. It wasn't until the orchestra started the overture that I truly understood what was happening. (Orchestra is a very generous title to give the ten fifteen-year-olds doing their absolute best to squeak out the score, but, bless their hearts.) I hadn't really thought about what would happen. I was going to see people singing, dancing, and acting live! If they were good, it would be amazing, and if they were bad, it would be AMAZING!

THE Haley Phillips, who played Dolly, was actually a friend of my brother. I had met her before and had even hung out with her a few times as the tag-along little brother. She was a senior and the star of the show, and I was practically her best friend. The other seventh graders had barely heard of her, so I was like, really cool!

Now, what you have to understand is that very few people in this town had an appreciation for the arts, let alone had a clue what *Hello, Dolly!* was. THE Haley Phillips, on the other hand, had somehow dedicated her life to music and performance. Somehow, despite the severe lack of arts education in this forgotten part of rural Texas, she had grown up singing, playing piano, and performing in almost every one of her high school productions. And she was good. Holy cow, she was amazing. Her comedic line delivery was up there with Carol Burnett, and she had a rich, sultry alto voice of a woman three times her age. This was just before Adele really burst onto the scene and gave the world what we all had been yearning for, but THE Haley Phillips was right here, selling it to a crowd in a nowhere town that barely cared.

I remember watching and thinking, "Wait, I was told THE Haley Phillips is playing Dolly, but this person who I'm watching is nothing like the girl I know," and this whole time, my seventh grade self was going back and forth like, "Is that her? That can't be her. It is her?" I was completely confused because she was that good. She was so transformed that I honestly had a hard time being certain.

After the performance was over and the final bows taken, the performers all went out to form a line at the exit to the auditorium. As my school's classes began to file out one by one, we had the chance to meet the cast and compliment them on their performances. As I walked out of the theatre and down the line, I finally reached her, the girl in the astonishingly ornate red and gold dress. It was Haley, and it had been her all along.

Truly, one of the coolest experiences I had ever had. Ever since then, I wanted to, no I *needed to* do just that. I wanted to be someone else. How powerful it must feel to have someone who knows you watch you and not recognize that it's even you. The skill to harness the mysterious power of transforming right in front of someone else's eyes. That aspect of performing is very alluring to me, but of course, over time I realize the power of live performance can be so much more meaningful.

The next year, eighth grade, was the year students were able to start their elective track. Up until now, we all had more or less the same core curriculum classes, but that was all about to change as we sorted ourselves into electives. This decision was huge, because it would set you up for your entire high school career. Were you going to be in the band? Would you sing in the choir? Or play a sport?

My brothers were both accomplished trumpeters throughout their school years. They played in every concert and marched at every football game. My parents had just expected that I would follow suit, relieved that they wouldn't have to purchase another trumpet. But I felt too cool for all of that. The Gonzales family had already been there and done that. I wanted to pave my own way, but I hadn't been sure which path in the road to choose until now!

I still remember *this* "coming out" to my parents. Though I didn't know it then, it would be a test run for a much bigger one later. We were out to eat one night at a Mexican restaurant, and the subject of picking my class schedule for the next year came up. I entered the chat gingerly with, "I'm not so sure I want to be in the band next year." My mother instantly fired back, "What do you mean you don't want to be in the band?!" I responded, "I think I'm going to sign up for theatre!" And then I awaited the blast from the self-destruct button I had just firmly pressed. Foreshadowing for the next time I dropped a bomb on my parents.

My parents begged me to reconsider, even threatening me that they would just override my decision and have the school place me in band. Even though I wasn't sure that was possible, I was scared to call their bluff. But, being incredibly strong-willed, I did things my way and still signed up for theatre. AH! I had been searching for a path for a while, though I didn't quite realize it. I was open to anything and on the lookout for a sign to smack me in the face. Something that would be *my* thing to separate me from my brothers. Something that I could call my own and give me a bit more sense of purpose. That openness gave me the courage to dip my toe into this new theatre world, and then later dive in head first.

I know it's something I love to do, but what happens in a theatre, in the room between the people on stage and off, is pure magic. On my first day in theatre, I was open to learning this whole new thing, but I hadn't realized the impact it could make on people. Seeing someone else's experience can help someone cope with their own, or understand a person they've hated, or even change their minds on a subject. But only if they are opened, by the performance, to receive the gift.

I tried to follow in THE Haley Phillips' footsteps as much as possible. I did theatre all throughout my high school years. I performed in about a dozen productions on that very stage in that very room where my life was forever changed. Creating my first artistic home and my first theatre family through those four years were the only things that helped my hormonal, angsty teenage self make it through the horrors that are high school. Of course, I ended up in the choir as well, just so I could get cast in the musicals. In a crazy spark of ingenuity, I even earned my required physical education credit from the drill team class, where I started to learn to dance.

After high school, I even attended the same college theatre program where THE Haley Phillips went. Though this college was much less than perfect, it was an incredible technique program that well equipped me for my acting career after graduation. I met lifelong friends that I continue to create theatre with today. In a fun way, I kind of owe all of my personal theatre history to THE Haley Phillips. Thank you, Haley. Thank you for this insane life I have chosen, where I am flat broke, people don't understand what I do, and I am constantly rejected and told I am not good enough. THANKS! No, really, thank you! I know I'll be forever grateful for such a powerful and life-changing gift.

With every project I do, whether as an actor, producer, or in a smaller capacity, I fall more and more in love with it. There is human connection with emotion and energy running between all parties involved. As much as I love television, movies, and books, and going on those journeys, they still never beat connecting in person with people in the same room. As Tracy Letts said during his Tony acceptance speech, "We are the ones who say it to their faces." We are charged with holding a mirror up to society, and for better or worse, show them how they are. We feel for them so that they know it is okay to feel. And as my beloved Judith Light once told me: "This is a customer service industry. Providing a higher and nobler service than all the rest!" That is why I keep going back.

My life has been transformed in such a profound way. I now wish to be the reason someone wants to do theatre with his or her life. I hope to be good enough, to one day open someone's heart to the possibility of the theatre being a home for them. I like to think that it has already happened, though of course, I'll probably never know. Maybe one child I've performed for was like, "Awesome! I want to do that." If ever I found out about that, it would make me the happiest person in the world.

We never know what might touch us. We don't know when something will pierce us deep into our core and light a torch we didn't know was dormant. What might swoop into our life and change the course of it beyond our wildest dreams. It could be a performance, God, a book, or a soulmate. I've found that the only conflicts created during these times is when we try to resist the tide. Diving in headfirst and swimming with the current will either get us to our new position or get us out of choppy waters faster. I've learned to keep myself open to these changes, these evolutions. I'd rather change than stay stagnant, though I know stagnation is the most comfortable place to be.

KEEP HONEST PART I

THE FIRST TIME I saw him was at my very first college party ever. It must've been the first week that classes began my very first semester. I was freshly introduced to a newfound freedom of being on my own for the first time, and I was very impatient for the next step in this crazy life. Pretty standard for the average eighteen-year-old. I quickly wanted to make every new person I came across my friend. I love meeting new people and learning about them, always have.

That particular week, I was so excited to actually be invited to a theatre party hosted at an upperclassman's apartment. College theatre politics are intense, to say the very least. Very few freshmen were invited to parties, but for some reason, I had been. Definitely not taking that chance for granted, I joined the other five or so invited freshmen and drove over to the upperclassman's off-campus apartment for my first real-life college party.

Heading over, we had no idea what to expect. The girls I was with all tried to dress "cool," whatever that meant, and were strategizing on how to get closer to a few of the junior boys who seemed to hold all of the status in the department at that time. They were good, and in this thing to win this thing. I figured if I stuck close to them, then I would be all right. I had no idea what I was going to do when I got there.

As soon as I walked in, a firecracker of a senior girl came up to me, grabbed my hand, and said, "Hey, you don't have a drink in your hand. Let's fix that!" She immediately whisked me into the kitchen, where I was handed a red cup and asked what I desired its contents to be. I stared back blankly for what seemed like forever, my mind racing. Was I going to be *hush* underage drinking? No, all I had to do was carry the drink, I didn't have to drink if I didn't want to. Oh GOD, WHAT IS EVEN A TYPE OF ALCOHOL? WHAT SHOULD I SAY?!

Luckily, the freshman girl beside me brightly chimed in with a sophisticated "Merlot!" and, not wanting to sound like I didn't know a single kind of alcohol, I repeated confidently, "Merlot!" The senior girl rolled her eyes for some reason and started pouring for us, and thus, I was handed my cup of red wine and sent to mingle with the other party-goers.

Merlot and I instantly began our search for the other freshmen who had been split from us during the alcohol sorting. We made our way through this dim, hot apartment into the living room, crowded with all of the loud, attention-seeking theatre majors. The air was thick with various talk about rehearsals, what classes folks were taking, and three or four people fighting for center stage.

He was sitting in a big chair flanked on either side by two other upperclassmen. They were talking, he was not, and immediately I was struck by his look. This boy looked like every single male vampire in cheesy young adult novels. You have to understand that the vampire craze had JUST hit, and *Twilight* and *True Blood* were everywhere. His cheekbones were sharp and high, competing with an even sharper jawline, set in the palest skin you could ever see on any human being. His skin contrasted with the most absolute jet black hair and big green eyes. Not quite evil-looking, but definitely held that bad-boy veil of mystery that would make any teenager go crazy.

We met, said hello, and then got to talking to everyone enjoying the party around us. He didn't say much, so I didn't really get to know him that night, but it was still a scene and a feeling that I'll always remember. Just an instant attraction? I wasn't even really sure what it was that I had discovered. But very soon after the moment in the living room, the police showed up due to a noise complaint (loud theatre majors), and I was suddenly in charge of escorting the underage drinkers back to campus safely without getting caught by the police. Scary time for a brand new college kid.

Later on that school year, this boy and I went on to be in a few classes together. In true theatre-major romance, we were in the beginner tap class together. Between all the flaps and shuffle-hop-steps, we got to know each other a bit. Though initially stand-offish and introverted, when he started to open up, I learned that he was a very sweet and kind individual with ambition and drive that one can only envy. He had been completing internships with his summers and getting real-world experience more than any of our peers at school. So, we bonded over our ambition and drive and became fast friends.

Then, one summer, he had begun an internship up north in Massachusetts, and I had been cast in a summer-stock production in Austin, Texas. During this time, technology was giving us more ways than ever to connect. Facebook videos and Skype were the big new things, so I was able to keep up with my friends through those methods. It made being away from my second serious theatre family bearable while we were spread across the country.

At that time in my life, I had never been to New York City. Though I felt a strong pull to the mythical land of dreams, I knew that I probably wouldn't be able to go there until I made the big move after graduation. During one of our video chats that summer, he proposed that if I fly up to Albany, he could pick me up, and then we would drive back together to school in Texas. He had taken his car for this job, needed to drive it back, and could use company for the long trip. We would make a kind of cross-country road trip out of it, seeing all of the sights: New York, Nashville, Washington, Philadelphia, and other places that I had wanted to see but never had the chance.

That was an offer I absolutely could not turn down, so you better believe I said yes so fast and got that plane ticket BOOKED! Over that road trip, we got to know each other a lot better. We got a lot closer and learned that we were much more similar than we thought. During this trip, without knowing it, we started falling for each other and realizing, "Hey, this is more than a friendship, more than a best friend-ship." It could very well be some sort of stronger attraction or destiny laid out for us. Though, since neither one of us was out, it was terrifying.

KEEP HONEST PART II

EVEN AFTER FALLING hard for this guy, I was still a little confused at this point in my life over what in the hell my sexuality was. Growing up in the conservative South, I was wrongly led to believe that being gay wasn't an option. It was more like gay people didn't even exist. There was very little sex education, so I had to rely on movies, friends, and the budding Internet to fill in gaps. Not the best resources, just saying. Let's all give a big hand to Texas for having a 100% heterosexual population with zero teen pregnancies. Because if you just don't acknowledge something, it clearly doesn't exist!

I sincerely remember the whole of puberty being summed up for us in a twenty-minute video, without even a question and answer session afterward. These video viewings were also segregated, of course. The boys watched the boy video, the girls watched the girl video. So, none of us male puberty-trekkers could possibly know what the female puberty-trekkers were going through, and vice versa. In high school, we spent exactly one lesson on the subject of "sex," said in quotes because I don't think the word "sex" was even mentioned once. The lesson was primarily focused on the names of different body parts and what sexually transmitted diseases and infections were.

Conversations at home were even worse. Being raised in a conservative, religious, Latine household meant that anything sex or body related was never discussed. NEVER! I somehow even learned that the topic shouldn't even be brought up. I innately knew that I was forbidden to even ask a question. The very best resource a kid should have when it comes to sexual education should be their parents.

They don't really talk about anything below the belt in The Bible Belt. So if I wasn't super into girls, I guess I was just supposed to be alone? I had a few girlfriends in high school, and I really did care for them, but I knew I just wasn't as "excited" as the other boys were. I wasn't that interested in sexually exploring with them, and I didn't really know why. I also started to come to terms with the fact that I *definitely* had crushes on a few dudes, too.

I didn't quite realize some were crushes because I was too young, like the older Boy Scout boy who taught me how to play cards on a camping trip when I was still a Cub Scout, or the athletic boy at church with the golden voice and perfectly symmetrical face. And then there were also ones that I really could not deny were a crush. The biggest of which, what I call my GAY-WAKENING, was JAMES MARSDEN. More specifically, James Marsden as Cyclops in the X-Men movies that were released right as I was entering those blessedly awkward puberty times.

Hailing from a comic book nerd household, the X-Men meant a lot to my brothers and me. The coolest leader of this epic team of evil-fighting mutants was Cyclops. Always one of my favorites, Cyclops was a strong, charismatic, cursed, and loyal upstanding man. When I saw the first movie, I fell more in love with the character, most likely due to the fact that he was portrayed by James Marsden. One of the most beautiful human beings to ever be on this planet. I was still perhaps a little too young to understand why I loved Cyclops from the movie so much, but I knew I wanted to be around him, or I wanted to BE him. Isn't that always the gay curse? Are we attracted to that man? Do we want to BE him? Or do we want to be WITH him? Or are we just petty jealous? OR ARE WE ALL OF THESE THINGS? Curse!

Flash forward to *X2* a few years later in 2003, and by then, there was no chance in me to deny that I had a full-blown crush on this man. He was just so cool, so beautiful, and definitely made me want to kiss on him, even without seeing his eyes. THAT'S how good James Marsden is at what he does, why I'll still watch anything he is in, and why he remains at the tippy-top of my celebrity crush list. Mix this with everything else going on in a teenager's life: school, college, moving out on my own, girlfriends, encounters with boys. How could I have even have the *time* to figure out my sexuality then?

Soon after the cross-country road trip, Matt and I began our relationship. It was still secret to pretty much everybody. Another thing you don't realize at first is that coming out is a never-ending process. But we figured our private Baptist university community and our very gossipy theatre department wasn't the environment we wanted to be in while we came out. I refused to expose myself for everyone's enjoyment. We decided to keep quiet for the time being, terrified of what would happen if our parents or families found out.

Though it was maybe a little unorthodox, I wouldn't trade how we handled this situation for anything. After the paparazzi spotlight through my brother's ordeal, I understood what it meant to be under the microscope. I knew that our relationship would be controversial and that people could say what they wanted, twisting it to whatever they needed it to be to feed their voyeurism. I knew I wanted to protect it until I was able to share our story on my own terms. When I understood who I was and what I wanted.

Then one night, I realized that I did not want to continue in this life without Matt by my side. I remember laying on his chest and bawling my heart out as I confessed that I did indeed love him. And my tears weren't out of fear of rejection or fear of the enormity of love. They were from how scared I was of what it would mean to go on in this world loving another man. What I would have to sacrifice, the judgments I would receive, and the prejudices that I would have to put up with, just to have him by my side. But I knew, even then, that it would be worth it.

At that time, gay marriage wasn't legal across the U.S. So, we figured we probably would never be able to get married. We weren't sure if we would ever be able to have a family of our own. Hell, at that point, we couldn't be certain that we would be able to have jobs, as people are still fired to this day just for being queer. That night, I wasn't able to handle all of those fears and the probable sacrifices, so I basically had an emotional breakdown for the first time in my life.

In true Matt fashion, he held me in his arms, comforted me, and let me know that he felt the same way. No matter what happened, he would be by my side, protecting me and making me feel safe, and we would get through whatever hardships came with our relationship together. From that day on, we have never looked back. And my gratitude for life grew even bigger with him. I am thankful for the courage he gave me to be myself and the honesty that I find in myself when I am with him.

KEEP LEARNING

Now LET'S TALK about the student loan crisis! Seriously, it's a huge problem, and I did not escape it, unfortunately. I sometimes daydream about some rich, benefactor sugar daddy coming in and forgiving my student loans, but so far that hasn't happened...yet! I am almost done paying them off, well ahead of most of my peers in the arts, and that makes me feel... better? I guess?

There is the whole starving artist, self-fulfilling prophecy that many seem to cling to for dear life, but I am of the belief that it doesn't have to be true. We are often led to believe by teachers, parents, and professors that we are not likely to make any money and will wait tables and live in poverty for the rest of our lives. And some of us cling to that vision of life as if it were some kind of noble duty, but not me. So ready or not, I'm going to pay these shits off!

I accrued this debt by attending a WAY overpriced private Baptist school, in Waco, Texas. Waco was THEN famous because of the Branch Davidian cult led by David

Koresh that led to one of the worst civilian/FBI debacles ever. NOW it's famous because of Chip and Joanna Gaines and their hit home makeover show *Fixer Upper* (and now their own television network). YAY!

I have no idea what the cost to attend this particular university is now, but when I attended, it was a whopping forty-five thousand dollars a YEAR! That brings us to a grand total of one hundred eighty thousand dollars for a four-year degree. Somebody, please check that math, because I got a Bachelor of Fine Arts and never had to take a math class, so I basically just guessed on that number. When choosing a degree that would make me the most money to make that huge investment worth it, I, of course, chose the famously high-earning major that is Theatre Performance. Luckily, due to my mother's strict insistence that we do well in school, and due to the low-income aid that was available to me at the time, I received an incredible sum of one hundred fifty thousand dollars in financial aid and scholarships, but DAMN, Y'ALL.

With this exorbitant price tag, the student body consisted mostly of very wealthy white kids, who came from long legacies of people who attended this same school throughout the generations. Many of these students' parents were very well-off or willing and able to go into extreme debt to provide their children with a movie-like college experience. These students had it ALL. Unlimited meal plans, new cars, the funds to join the expensive fraternities and sororities, and then, in most cases, an allowance of hundreds of dollars a week for just whatever else they might need. Here I was, a poor Latino, who at the age of eighteen had roughly the same look and size of a twelve-year-old, dropped into a BRAVO reality show for the rich and famous... and white!

Being ever resourceful (Go Slytherin!), I quickly infiltrated this wealth network that I knew nothing about, by doing what I know how to do best: seem non-threatening, dazzle them with a smile, and make them laugh with my jokes, quick wit, and wacky antics. All ways we "lesser haves" are taught to interact with those we have no business interacting with. I helped them with their homework, showed them how to spend less money daily so that their four hundred dollar allowance for the week would actually last all week (EYEROLL), and even showed them how to apply for a *GASP* job! I was honestly surprised by how much they appreciated me teaching them how to stack discounts on clothes or go grocery shopping: extreme couponing edition.

By bringing them some real value in a kind and non-judgmental way, I was able to make true connections with so many wonderful people. I still silently marveled at their whimsically WASPY lives, but soon many of them started to help me in my journey, realizing that I didn't have a direct credit card to my parents' money like they did. As if my parents would even have that kind of money to begin with! Thankfully, these students were mostly kind and compassionate. They realized they were blessed with the funds, and most didn't mind sharing when they could.

There were so many people who helped me buy food, get gas, or shared their allowance with me so that I could join them for a movie. I had my first glimpse at this different lifestyle. My mouth dropped in awe as I learned what North Face meant, and who that girl Lulu Lemon was. Surprisingly almost everyone was open, loving, kind, and willing to give. Well, the students, at least. I had a very hard time with the faculty, especially those that ran the theatre department. But what theatre kid doesn't?

While the theatre department gave me great, top-notch acting training, they were stuck in the Dark Ages about how to actually make a career as a performing artist. Sadly, this is a fact that most university performance programs struggle with, even today. Added on top of that was a healthy dose of racism that kept them focused on the white students who could play all the roles instead of the brown students who would have to wait until the "brown play" came up, or—even worse—the black students who would have been entirely forgotten if they hadn't been used, at least once each, to lend their "Blackness" to some horribly offensive role. The professors were very reluctant to change or even learn the best programs or best practices to keep the information they were giving students as up-to-date as possible. Professors insisted on the horrific jewel-tone dresses and shirts as the only acceptable audition outfit. Or that you absolutely needed to pay a thousand dollars for a headshot that looked exactly like a high school senior photo. And don't get me started on the push-back we students received when we tried to get more recordings of our performances for future audition submissions. They were unwilling to equip students with the best possible tools to go out into the field.

Due to the rise of the Internet and social media, I quickly caught on to what I was missing in academia. Again, ever resourceful and with an insatiable desire to grow, learn, and develop, I began researching everything I could about the industry. Once you learn what is happening this very instant in your field, you are able to make better decisions and prepare yourself for the future. Not only are you able to spot upcoming trends or yesterday's news, but you are also able to cultivate your own network. I was able to reach out to those already established while also connecting with my peers on the rise in different parts of the country. We all were able to help and support each other.

Through this research and by following in an upperclassman's footsteps, I learned of a summer training program that took place in NEW YORK CITY. I had only ever been to New York City once before, for exactly twenty hours, on that crazy cross-country road trip I took with my best friend. Even better, this training program had a few scholarships to offer, so it wasn't completely off the table. It was a long shot, but the worst that could happen was they'd say no, and I would spend that summer slinging crab claws at the local Red Lobster to pay for the next semester of school.

I submitted on a whim, and like most things in the entertainment industry, I forgot about it. If I didn't get it, I wouldn't hear, and if I did, someone would reach out. I'd already learned to let go of things at this point. But then, one Tuesday afternoon, I received a random call, and lo and behold, it was this program offering me a spot! I was so grateful but remained reserved until I had all the details. It's not like I was sure I could pull off a flight, housing, food, and tuition to the program. After the initial thanks and appreciation, the woman on the other end of the line had one final piece of news: Due to some generous donors and my financial need, they had also selected me for a scholarship covering almost the entire cost of the program. Now the floodgates of gratitude opened in my eyeballs.

I immediately let my close friends know and started planning how I was going to pull this off. The program was only about two months away. With my work-study program, I could cover the cost of the flight and some food if I stuck to just one meal a day. "Three meals a day is for the WEAK!" I willed myself into believing. I knew some folks in New York City that had just graduated, and three of them so graciously offered me at least a floor in their apartment for one week. My total time in New York City would span three weeks, so this worked perfectly, and one even had a couch! This was going to work! I was going to SPRINGBOARDNYC!

SpringboardNYC is still around today and is still one of the best summer intensive programs for college actors to prepare for the real world. This program is part of the American Theatre Wing, the institution that hosts the Tony Awards, and hosts a myriad of incredible resources for budding theatre world professionals. For two weeks, college actors are brought in for all-day training. There are classes, masterclasses, and mock audition scenarios all run by the top people in the industry. Current Broadway directors, actors, musical directors, and more came to work with us. Even that year's Tony nominees came and sat with us and answered whatever questions we had during the craziness that is Tony season. After the day of classes, every evening all of the SpringboardNYC students went to see shows all around the city. Seriously, every night we were at a Broadway show, or we saw the incredible immersive performance *Sleep No More*, which was relatively new at the time and a hot commodity.

It all culminated in the biggest night in American theatre: the Tony Awards ceremony. That's right, we got to go to the Tony Awards!

SpringboardNYC was one of the most life-changing experiences I've ever had. I worked with top music director Seth Rudetsky on my audition cuts of songs, studied scene work with director and Tony-winning choreographer Kathleen Marshall, got to have an intimate question-and-answer session with Judith Light and plenty of other esteemed artists that I had only been able to follow online for years. All for one-one hundredth of the cost of my so-called university education.

Perhaps even more valuable than these lessons with the professionals were the "real world" classes and resources that the program creators developed. They taught us the best ways to find an apartment in New York City, what each neighborhood was like, what expenses we could expect, and even how to do our taxes as an artist. Each of these things being something that the university education system wouldn't even *think* to teach. Yet all were necessary lessons to even have a shot at being successful.

Somewhere along the way, I believe society went very wrong by placing too much stock in the higher education system. Growing up, we were led to believe that we could only be successful if we went to college. Most of us took on tens of thousands of dollars in debt to get a mediocre education, the bulk of which was in subjects we would never use in our careers. And still, even after forking over all of this money, we still weren't taught how to fill out a ballot, file our taxes, purchase a home, or set up a retirement account.

My hope is that the next generations find real knowledge elsewhere in the world. The best real-world lessons I learned were taught nowhere near my college.

I also made lifelong friends with my fellows in the SpringboardNYC program and have gotten to cheer them on throughout their journeys. Many of them are still working in the theatre to this day, and some of them have already made their Broadway debuts. This program has been around for years, and I hope it continues forever. It is an invaluable resource for so many theatre artists in training. If you or anyone you know is a college theatre student, please point them to this program.

The truly life-changing lesson I learned that summer was just how small the theatre world really is. All of these teachers and students came from the same types of backgrounds as me. We are all part of this artistic world that we love and understand when so many people don't. All of these huge celebrity giants were really just people. Approachable, loving, and willing to help the next up-and-coming artists on their path with whatever knowledge they could pass on. I know I've been extremely lucky to be the recipient of this knowledge, so I will be damned if I don't turn right around and pass it along to others as well. I have to. It's the very least I'm called to do for being so fortunate.

And let me start the passing of that knowledge with the single greatest through-line for all of these professionals, even at the height of their careers. It was one simple thing. They all expressed how important it was that they continue their education throughout the rest of their lives. They all proclaimed how an artist should never stop learning. They never stop working on their craft. Whether that be in keeping up with voice lessons, acting coaching, or even just learning other skills or hobbies that will make them a more well-rounded human being. Every single one of them had the humility to admit that they did not know all that they needed to know, no matter how many accolades they had been given. Never EVER stop learning!

KEEP HUMBLE

I THINK THE world is really trying to tell me something. Have you caught on yet? We all have weaknesses, and the greatest battle of your life will be identifying those and keeping them in check. Making sure they don't flare up and destroy your current ventures. One of my greatest weaknesses, overconfidence, can also be one of my greatest strengths. However, I've discovered you oftentimes get the most out of a situation by humbling yourself.

I find it funny how I'm reminded time and time again to stay humble, thankful, and to not expect anything or feel like I deserve anything. Sometimes that overconfidence can swell into entitled arrogance, and we all need to keep that in check, especially the younger we are. The summer after graduating college really helped me learn to check that overconfidence and keep a larger perspective for the rest of my life.

You know how you hear about crazy groups of hippies in the 1970s that would go out in the middle of nowhere for weeks at a time and do God knows what? Play music, sing songs, drink and smoke anything they could get their hands on, and spend sweaty nights in various pairs, threes, or groups. Think of Burning Man, or Bonnaroo for all of you fellow Millennials / Gen Z folks. It's the young, dumb, broke, and horny artist's dream. Just getting together with a bunch of super brilliant artists, like yourself, better than yourself, and then just creating art. Well, this magical land exists. And I challenge anyone who says that the Williamstown Theatre Festival is not the best damn artist commune out there.

The summer after I graduated college in 2012, I had the incredibly lucky chance to attend the Williamstown Theatre Festival in Williamstown, Massachusetts. Or as those in the know call it lovingly: WTF. Co-founded and led for its first thirty years by the legendary Nikos Psacharopoulos (WHAT A NAME, MAN), the Williamstown Theatre Festival is the resident theatre company that resides every summer on the campus of Williams College in Williamstown. Now, throughout the school year, Williams College is a very respectable, yet fairly small, college. There is one street on the entire campus, with a coffee shop, ice cream shop, pizza place, and drug store. (Or is it "shoppe?" Williamstown definitely is the type of place that would call them "shoppes.")

However, when summertime comes and the students of Williams College go back home, the entire campus is invaded by hundreds of actors, directors, playwrights, musicians, and the hardest working techies and production staff I've ever seen. These people live and breathe theatre with every fiber of their soul. They work all summer to get these productions up in record times, and achieve twenty-four-hour changeovers. That means loading out an entire professional musical and loading in another in twenty-four hours. INSANITY! The WTF shows are the only things that matter to these people.

One of the best things that WTF has going for it is the amount of well-established artists and celebrities who got their start there, or that continue to come back occasionally to do work. Each summer, WTF hosts a list of Broadway's who's who, but also many folks you'd never expect. For instance, the summer I was there had Justin Long, Leslie Mann, Sam Rockwell, Philip Seymour-Hoffman, and Bradley Cooper, among others. Remember, the entire campus and town could fit in a snow globe. So oftentimes you rub shoulders or work with these folks on stage, in a classroom, or just at the local pub, coffee shop, or party.

Now, for fledgling student theatre-makers who wish to attend this fabled festival, WTF offers what they call an acting apprenticeship program. While the program is supposed to focus the majority of the time on acting training, it doesn't always work that way for all of the acting apprentices. Basically, they get hundreds of college juniors and seniors to apply with only about forty eventually accepted into the program. Once selected, these apprentices have to pay their way for room, board, travel, etc. in order to spend the entire summer working on show crews, taking classes with famous artists, doing the majority of the hard labor, and if they're lucky, getting some really rad performance experiences and building an awesome network. All practices that now border on being exploitative, but it was kinda all we had then.

I am proud to say that it was by far the best summer I have ever had, and probably will ever have. I was sequestered in the middle of the Massachusetts countryside abyss creating art alongside some of the most brilliant, famous minds of our time. Many people look on the WTF apprenticeship as a kind of "pay to play" vibe, given the fact that the apprenticeship without a scholarship will run someone anywhere from three to five thousand dollars, but it is honestly what you make of it. Being from a no-art, small Texas town, I was definitely going to make the most of it. Also, because it cost a lot of money, even with scholarships, I knew I didn't really have a choice. Plus, unlike the majority of wealthier theatre kids, I wasn't afraid of work. I was willing to put my head down, pay my dues, and learn as much as I could.

For the first part of the summer, I was assigned to be on the backstage run crew for a production of *The Importance of Being Earnest*, directed by the distinguished Niles Crane himself, David Hyde Pierce. Our primary job was to serve as a fifteen-person "automatic set track." As in, they couldn't put a motorized track into the space to move the train of set pieces, so they made fifteen of us apprentices line up and push a three-ton set across the stage. AND WE ABSOLUTELY LOVED IT! We got to hang out with bomb-ass stage managers, who are still my friends to this day, David Hyde-Pierce, and the one and only Tyne Daly!

Every day, Tyne would regale us with stories and wisdom about the biz, as she sat far off-stage waiting to make her entrance. We would all sit, bright-eyed and bushy-tailed on the ground, in all black, like some sort of Tyne cult, hanging on each and every one of her words. I honestly learned so much from that wonderful force of a woman. Her storied career had taught her much, and she was more than willing to share all she had learned.

The most memorable event during the run of that show occurred in the second week of performances. Well set in our stage crew tracks, some of us may have gotten a bit too comfortable. That comfort that comes once you've learned your job and rest on your laurels a bit too much, losing the absolute focus. This lack of focus caused us to be a little less careful and eventually led to disaster, as it often does.

My best friend on the crew was Amy. Hilarious, joyous, and a fountain of youthful energy, Amy is the best. We grew close fast and were inseparable on that crew. Never not laughing and always making the most of the long hours of the festival. One fateful day, we were executing the big intermission move of the set. All twenty or so people lined up and synced to push the three tons of set to the opposite side of the theatre.

Having fun, and throwing ourselves into the platforms, we may have gotten a touch distracted, and next thing I knew, Amy's foot started to disappear under the set. I swear I saw her life flash before my eyes, as the wheel of the platform started eating her toes, and then more and more of her foot. In an instant, I screamed at the top of my lungs, "HOLD! STAGE LEFT ONE, TWO, THREE!!" And in one of the most inspiring moments of human connection and the language of theatre people, everyone immediately changed course and started pushing the set from whence it came. Not one person questioned why a lowly acting apprentice started calling the shots. They knew there must have been a reason and immediately joined to help. Moments later, Amy's foot was released from the prison of weight, and her life was spared. While her foot was broken, she was not crushed, and she lived to laugh about it many, many days later. It was crazy scary. And further proof that I am amazing in emergency situations and can save people's lives! Cast me in an *ER* reboot guys! MY BODY IS READY!

Later in the summer, I would be thrown into a crazy role as the dresser to the male lead on the new mainstage musical. Some of you might know a little forgotten show that was *Far From Heaven*. After WTF, it had a shorter Off-Broadway run at Playwright' Horizons in New York City. It was based on the 2002 film of the same name, starring Julianne Moore, Dennis Quaid, and Patricia Clarkson. Clarkson also happened to be starring at WTF that summer in the Bradley Cooper vehicle version of *The Elephant Man*. I hadn't seen the film version of *Far From Heaven*, but apparently it was groundbreaking in its portrayal of the closeted 1950s husband that is struggling with his sexuality. Hot. This new musical version starred Kelli O'Hara, pre-Tony win but after Tony-deserved performances, and the "Not Quite Yet Mother Panty Dropper" Steven Pasquale.

Well, due to exhaustion at WTF, because apprentices literally worked twenty to twenty-six hours a day, Steve's original dresser walked straight into a glass wall and shattered it, breaking his arm in the process. I swear to God, you can't make this shit up. He was so damn tired, he just casually smashed into an entire glass wall while simply walking, shattering the glass as well as his body. While injured, there was no way he would be able to keep up with all of the quick changes, so they rushed to find a replacement apprentice that wasn't currently assigned to a crew.

So… I had to immediately step in to help with Steve's

THIRTEEN quick changes without any prior rehearsal...
during a paid audience matinee performance. I was incredibly terrified, but I knew I couldn't let it show. Luckily,
Steve is a great guy and helped me as much as he could,
and he never yelled or even spoke up when I obviously did
something wrong. Very different from the demeanor he can
initially give off to those who just meet him.

My favorite moment from the entire situation happened
right before the half-hour call of that performance. While
hustling around the dressing room, making sure all the pieces
were there, I suddenly felt someone grab my arm and pull
me to the side. I looked up to see THE (now, since 2015,
Tony Award-winning) Kelli O'Hara. I was so stunned that
my eyes had trouble focusing on her face, a condition that I
saw her register immediately. As sweet as you can imagine,
she gave me the biggest pep talk right then and there. She
thanked me for stepping in and acknowledged that I was
just as important to the show as she was, and that everyone
was there with me and for me, in case I needed anything. I
never get star-struck, but her sheer kindness and awesomeness made me want to cry. And just like that, armed with the
O'Hara courage, I executed all thirteen quick changes that I
had never done before, for the lead actor, and the show ran
smoothly for the rest of the run.

After a summer of working my ass off, WTF definitely
saved the best for last. During the last month of summer,
I was informed that I was actually going to be *in* the last
mainstage of the season. WHAT?! I was actually going to be
on stage, in scenes of a WTF show?! I'm pretty sure I didn't
even believe it until the show closed.

That show was *WHADDABLOODCLOT!!!* A new world-premiere play by Katori Hall (*The Mountaintop, Tina: The Tina Turner Musical*). A handful of apprentices were chosen to play various ensemble roles and to help out with set changes and a certain fight scene that breaks out in Harlem. It was a blast and a time I will definitely treasure for the rest of my life. The play is hilarious and an amazing story of a wealthy white woman who learns the hard way just how racist she is. The main cast were all veterans of television and Broadway. I learned so much from them every day; it was incredible. I honestly can't put into words all the feelings I am feeling right now, but know that I will forever be grateful. All of the apprentices in that show knew that we had something very special given to us. I love you all.

My summer at WTF taught me more than any other time in my life. In those three short months, I learned how to never stop working. I learned that I could compete and play alongside artists who had successfully made a career doing what I wanted to do. I had the chance to pay my dues and humbly accept any task or job asked of me, because I knew that it would put me in a good light and that my work ethic would win people over. And it did! As, on the final day of the festival, I moved to New York City with a network of about one hundred theatre-makers that I knew I could call upon for help, or that would be willing to work with me. That wanted to work with me.

I think it's easy for those just out of college to feel like they are prepared, or like they know and can do it all. I'm here to remind you that you never will know it all, especially at that time of your life. I'd caution anyone who thinks they are above doing the less glamorous work that happens out of the spotlight in any industry. Humility and dedication to the greater work never goes unnoticed. It's always paid back in lessons learned or advancement to a new level. Sometimes you really do need to put your head down and blow them away with the job you've been given.

KEEP HONEST PART III

Now FULLY ACCEPTING that I was gay, I added Matt to my party roster in this role-playing game simulation we call life. Also, a new secret potential was unlocked for me. I started to appreciate other parts of myself that I was taught to be ashamed of my entire life. Parts of myself that I had subconsciously kept hidden, in order to obtain the ideal toxic masculinity I was taught I should possess. It was a trait I never had, but sometimes I had to pretend as a means of survival. It was the first role I would play, only this one was out of pure necessity.

I loved giving into these truer parts of my being that I had suppressed for such a long time. I am emotional, crying at most movies and at almost every single live stage performance, even if it's not particularly good. Especially if it's a musical. As soon as the first down beat hits, I'm usually overwhelmed and completely with the cast from the get. I laugh at every joke and cry with every emotional moment or song. I'm the best audience member there ever was.

I could also start fully embracing my nerdy self to the highest level. Even if people gave me strange looks when I tried to explain all the evidence that supported my case that Mr. Fuji played a huge role in the creation of Mewtwo (a fan theory that I strongly subscribed to, that would later go on to be confirmed as true in the official Pokémon canon).

More than anything, I allowed myself to fall in love. Matt made me feel completely safe to be my full, honest self. Eventually, we would come out to folks gradually, and then never stop. Because you never do stop coming out. It starts with one person, then a few more people, then all of your friends, then your family, then your workplace, online, and then to everyone in the future forever. It's one big, long-running negotiation that I, as a gay man, unfortunately have to keep coming back to over and over again.

I wish more allies understood just how much of a burden this process can be. How it is a constant program our brain computers are running in the background as we try and navigate everyday life activities. We keep a running list of who we've come out to, who we haven't, who is safe, who is not. And we can become remarkably accustomed to keeping these lists straight without slipping up. These ninja acrobatics cost us sheer mental and emotional energy when we could put that energy toward other things instead. Years of productivity lost unnecessarily in the name of survival.

While working at a Starbucks, I carefully let my manager know by requesting time off for my boyfriend's birthday. She grimaced, but it turned out to be the annoyance of having to find a replacement for my shift. I eagerly expressed my gayness to my new fellow servers in New York City as we pretended not to hear the calls of our manager to run food to tables. In that instance, I grew closer to my new friends! And I calmly and evenly told my mother, as gently as possible, fully aware of what would happen, and was unsurprised when she accused me of doing something terrible to HER.

Each moment of revelation is carefully calculated, all variables and threats weighed and balanced in real time, so as to minimize potential harm and yet get the information across. Over time, these negotiations became easier. With less and less to lose if a new person wasn't cool with it, I would have all the leverage to not back down and stand my ground. For all my gaybies, young in their coming out journey, I think this is a more tangible understanding of "it gets better."

Our friends and family would have mixed responses, but most were positive. It was a huge sign that things were changing for the better with Obama in office at the time. Most people who had negative reactions got there with time, and luckily, none of ours were the horror stories that still happen to this day. I wasn't thrown out anywhere or called names; I was just "prayed for" a lot. I'll take it!

I grew up in the church and still consider myself a Christian, although I'm not so sure I believe in most organized churches. But, I understood the difficulty of these people trying to understand and still be loving. I understood that they were wrestling with the purer version of God's love in the Bible, against what they had been told by pastors their whole lives. Their pastors were men who had taken it upon themselves to translate the word of the Lord to their congregations and pass judgment upon anyone they choose.

As the nation continued to get more involved and started to evolve, we saw huge sweeping legislation to protect LGBTQ+ people and give us some of the freedoms and rights that other heterosexual couples had all along. You know, just a few basics like being able to get married legally, minimal familial rights for queer parents, and anti-discrimination laws to help protect us from not getting fired from our jobs for no good reason. We started winning battles that had been fought for decades and decades by generations before us.

Now, this country still has a very long way to go in that fight, and I know that in my lifetime I'll never stop fighting. But, slowly our world began to accept us more and more each day. And a future with Matt came into focus. One that I would never have thought could be. With these new circumstances, I started to believe that maybe one day we could be married to one another. Maybe one day we would have a wonderful family of our own, and friends, and live in New York City with a wonderful community of love surrounding us. With all of these recent gifts, I fully understand the responsibility I have to be completely honest about who I am. I have a responsibility to live my life in truth so that others who may struggle like I did can see it *is* possible!

KEEP CLOSE

THE DAY THAT WTF ended, I had no idea what was going to happen in my life. It was the first time in my life I had no plan laid out or calendar of events for my immediate future. I had my two suitcases, one pillow, knew I was going to New York City, and that's about it. Thankfully, I knew how to work my new network of folks to help me out.

One of my apprentice friends had brought his car to the festival and was kind enough to give me a ride to the city on his way back to New Jersey. I scored this ride only the day before I was set to leave. I honestly don't know how I would have gotten to the city otherwise. I also had two friends from college who had moved to the city together at the start of the summer and agreed to let me stay on their couch for a couple of weeks.

Victoria and Karina were two of the very first friends I made in college. They were both in my class in the theatre department, so of course, we will forever be joined. They had become best friends themselves, seemingly on the first day of college, and they remain ride-or-die for each other to this very day. They moved to New York City a few months before me and had secured a shoebox, two hundred fifty-square foot studio from an older college alum.

This apartment was literally just a small rectangle with a quarter alleyway kitchen off to the side, and a small, blush-pink-tiled bathroom. That bathroom is quintessential old New York, and WE LOVED IT! Victoria and Karina had two twin beds that they placed in opposite corners facing each other. They would go to sleep at the same time and wake up at the same time. After four years in college, I think you are better suited for, and even accustomed to, close room-mate living. I cannot even imagine that kind of setup now.

My first week in the city, I stayed on their couch. And then the next week, Matt joined me in the city, so we both stayed on their couch for a few weeks. That's right, we had four fully-grown adults sharing this minuscule space in New York City just trying to make it. I regret that it wasn't a super fun party-house environment that we probably should have taken advantage of, like teenagers all bunking in the same cabin with no counselors around. Unfortunately, we were all scrambling to find jobs, apartments, and the money to order Thai food from around the corner that would last at least three meals. Although it's much less glamorous, we were probably more like the four grumpy grandparents all sharing a bed in *Charlie and the Chocolate Factory*.

Once Matt and I found our own first New York City apartment, I began working as a server at a restaurant in Times Square: the famous Junior's. It was a huge restaurant with an old-timey diner theme. While the food is way overpriced and mediocre, they are known for their cheese-cake, which is underpriced and the best cheesecake you'll ever eat. I *love* cheesecake. If cheesecake asked for my hand in marriage, I would immediately buy it a Tiffany's ring, book a plane to Paris, write the pope, and... I don't really know where I was going with that metaphor, but I just know I, like, really love cheesecake!

While working a late shift one night, I received an email asking me to come in for an interview for a production assistant gig on a then-popular web series known as *Submissions Only*. If you do not know *Submissions Only*, you should. In an era of *Smash* and *Glee*, actors slash writers slash film makers Andrew Keenan-Bolger and Kate Wetherhead sought to tell a more realistic story about life as New York City actors. And I must say, if you are, are planning to be, or have ever been a New York City actor, it is a MUST. SEE. It primarily focuses on the auditioning aspect of the biz and how awkward the whole premise of "auditioning" is. You'll laugh, you'll cry, and some things will hit so close to home, you will think they *must* have been filming your life in secret.

Submissions Only was set to start filming its third season in a few weeks, and they were looking for some extra production assistants to help out. At the time, I had no idea how they had gotten my contact information, but I was so stoked! I shoved the rest of my break burger into my mouth, paid a friend to do my side work, and quickly worked to move my last tables outta there so I could get home and get ready for this interview. Back in my younger days, an internship on the set of an extremely low budget web series was clearly much more important than waiting tables so I could afford rent and/or food!

So, the next morning I arrived at the interview a little nervous. Being a fan of the show, I really wanted the chance to work alongside these people, but I didn't know anything about being on a film set. I mean, I did bring up the one film production class I took in eighth grade, but that was with an outdated digital camera that still used floppy disks. I was adamant, though, that I was a team player, responsible, and willing to learn everything I would need.

And in a lightning strike of luck, they accepted me on to their team! Hooray! I had just graduated, moved to New York City, and all of a sudden I found myself joining this team of incredibly talented, established, well-known actors. I was so over-the-moon excited! I had infiltrated this group and would be working hand-in-hand with the pros.

Throughout the filming of season three, I became friends with the cast and crew, bonding over long days, and the passion we all shared to make this project the best it could be. I got to see these artists work so seamlessly and easily, even while overcoming challenges like transporting equipment through the city or blowing out several lightbulbs in one day. I soaked up every single second of it as I was holding a light reflector about an inch away from their faces, and about a half inch out of the frame of the camera. It was the most fun masterclass I could have ever asked for.

My duties included the most glamorous tasks that are involved in any filming production, including but not limited to: carrying heavy equipment, setting up said heavy equipment, and holding said heavy equipment for extended periods of time without moving, sometimes in freezing cold weather. Kate, Andrew, Neal, and Kyle: if you are reading this, I truly thank you all from the bottom of my heart for every second.

I will forever have two favorite days from this shooting process. The first is when we shot a scene at (Tony Award-winning and sister to Andrew) Celia Keenan-Bolger's apartment. The scene was a fun game night involving most of the cast, so we set it up in Celia's living room. She graciously gave her brother the go-ahead to do whatever we needed to do, and over the course of the day, we absolutely destroyed this poor girl's apartment.

We rearranged every piece of furniture she had, we possibly broke some blinds at one point, we moved anything smaller than a shoebox to a completely different place, we completely maxed out the apartment's power grid, and in a terrifying moment, we even almost caught the place on fire when a light was knocked over. It slammed into the ground, shattering the lightbulb with a bright blue spark. It was insane.

Then, after the long, long hours of shooting the fun scene, we realized we had to try and put everything back exactly how we found it. Something we probably should have kept in mind from the start. Kate was the leader of this mission, deciphering the "before" photos she had intelligently taken, and barking orders as to what went where. The rest of us frantically scurried around in a flurry of tidying, desperately trying to make sense of Kate's words while in an exhausted haze from the day. Good times!

My second favorite shoot day was filming a little scene with three-time Tony Award-winner Judith Light. If you ever have an opportunity to be in the same room as this woman, never let a moment pass without soaking up her light. I know it sounds like a cliché, bad pun, nausea-inducing metaphor, but I swear to God, that wonderful woman actually exudes the spirit of light and wonder in whatever room she is in!

She so graciously was down to shoot a quick little scene on this show that would do nothing for her career or wallet. And not only that, she came more than prepared! She was fully memorized. She brought a suitcase filled with costume options. She also brought a handful of her own props. And when the cameras started rolling she had CHOICES! Judith gave everything she could, as if she were on set for a huge blockbuster movie. That is the generous spirit I hope to have in my life. #TeamJudithLight

The *Submissions Only* team gave me my first real introduction to the film production world. I worked around it all day every day, so I got to soak up all that knowledge that would make me a better collaborator for the next sets I would be on as an actor. I learned how shots are set up, the different lenses and their uses, all about sound engineers, and how actors act for a camera. When filming for season three was wrapping up, I also got my next gig, which would be very similar.

One of my fellow interns on set was on a path to become a Broadway stage manager. She had been recruited to be a production assistant at *Once* on Broadway and enlisted a few of us to join her. It was definitely another one of those right place, right time, right connection things, but when they happen, you say, "YES!" and count your blessings.

Once was based off of the indie film about two musicians struggling to make it in Ireland. The main song, "Falling

Slowly," would go on to win the Oscar for Best Original Song, and thus a musical adaptation was certain. I also feel like there could have been a little divine intervention that led me to this particular show.

When *Once* opened on Broadway in 2012, an alumnus from my college, Elizabeth A. Davis, was in the original cast. Not only is Elizabeth a great actress and singer, but she's also an accomplished violin player. After all, a musical about musicians works best when the actors are their own orchestra, thus *Once* would start a wave in the theatre world of the "actor-musician." The full cast played all of the instruments in the show, as well as sang, danced, and everything else. Each member of the cast could play multiple instruments, and the swings needed to be able to play all of them. Guitar, piano, violin, cello, bass, banjo. It was incredible.

With Elizabeth's perfect skill set, she had been picked up by the show early in its development, performing in previous iterations before the show made its move to Broadway. Elizabeth was even nominated for a Tony Award for her performance. This was the first time in a LOOONG time that a graduate from my university had gotten to this level of a theatrical career. It was a celebration for us alums everywhere. And, even though she left the show just before I joined the *Once* team, it was always a special bonus I kept with me. I got to be the second alum to work on the production.

Little did I know how quickly I would become part of the *Once* family. As a production assistant (PA), I was a glorified lackey for the stage managers. Every night, I "worked," I was onstage assistance for them during the special pre-show and intermission portions of the production. The entire show was set in an Irish pub, and before the show and at intermission, the bar was a real working bar that audience members were invited to enjoy.

We'd let them onstage, they could purchase and enjoy drinks, and even be up close to the actors while they played and performed a few songs. My job was to be an extra hand for crowd control. Obviously, we couldn't fit the entire audience onstage, so I would help regulate the flow of the crowd. I also would answer any questions, stop audience members from taking photos, and be on the lookout for any crazies that may try to touch the performers or the instruments.

The job was easy, but for a new struggling actor who dreamt of one day performing on a Broadway stage, it was the BEST job ever! While not on stage, I got to hang in the green room, chatting with the cast and crew. I'd watch how they did their jobs day in and day out. It's one thing to run a show a few times for a few weeks. It's entirely different to do the show eight times a week for YEARS. Those were the skills I craved to discover.

My favorite part of the work day was the warm-up. Before every show, all of the actors would come on stage and warm up together. Every day, I would arrive a little early so I wouldn't miss it. After saying hello to the doorwoman, signing in, and grabbing my walkie talkie, I'd dash up the stairs to the stage to watch them warm up. They'd occasionally have jam sessions, which were such a treat. When all of these artists were getting ready to do what they love, what I love, it was truly inspiring, and of course, they were always supportive and willing to share tips and tricks to the young actors who were PAs.

Some of the cast at the time had been with the show for over two years, and yet they were never stale. Watching them keep it fresh, add different nuances, and still love the show after doing it over and over again was remarkable. Along with all the tedious everyday things they do while working on a Broadway show, they still gave their all over and over to tell this beautiful story. I got to watch and learn, and watch and learn.

All these little opportunities were baby steps that helped propel me to where I eventually wanted to be. Another wish that I'd like to declare to anyone, artist or not, who is trying to make something of themselves or achieve something great, would be to remember that your journey is a marathon, not a sprint. Sure, some people get head starts, but we all can finish. You have to be in it for the long haul. Get close to those who are where you want to be. Being in the same room with these powerhouses taught me the lessons college could never. I wasn't paid much for these lessons and sometimes I had to make sacrifices in order to get into the room with the people I wanted to be with. But those sacrifices are always worth it.

KEEP LISTENING

IT'S COMMONLY BELIEVED that the most important key to great acting is listening. Teachers will often recite the mantra, "acting is reacting." Anybody can recite lines and put some feeling behind them, or incorporate a wacky character choice. These things are much simpler to do than the harder part. The bulk of a good actor's work is what they do when they aren't speaking. But it's not just looking at your scene partner and hearing the words they say. It's so very much more than that.

It's taking in everything they communicate to you. Not just with their words, but with their body, tone, and inflection. Then effortlessly letting that communication affect you in a way that is most natural to you under the given circumstances of the scene. Audiences can see this active listening. They can interpret the wheels turning in an actor's head and the lightning-fast reactions that fly across an actor's face. These happen faster than if they were planned.

And when we aren't listening, all hell can break loose.

This is when mistakes and bloopers happen. Sometimes as an actor, when you are performing your one-hundredth performance of the same show, it can be so tempting to go on autopilot and zone out. Your muscle memory can take care of the blocking and the lines, but if anything out of the ordinary is slightly off, you can get caught off guard. If your scene partner says a line completely differently this performance, it wakes you up, but you weren't listening, so you have no idea what they just said. You have no idea where you are in the show or what to say next. You weren't listening, really.

I believe this type of active listening makes a scene feel real. It draws in an audience and makes them completely forget that they are watching two people acting, but rather they are watching these characters as if they were there. The audience is lost in the emotional energy flowing between them and spilling out onto us. This focused listening is how we communicate in real life, so it makes sense that it brings so much emotional weight with it onto the stage.

Or, I guess I should say it's how we all *should* communicate in real life. We should be listening with every fiber of our being, taking in everything someone is trying to tell us. I find that people as a whole have a harder and harder time listening lately. In an age of the Internet, we almost don't have to. It's far too easy to find your own echo chamber in a Facebook group and continue shouting into the void. Or firing off a text, as if we can't even lend our voice most of the time. Hell, I'd even argue that emojis do a better job communicating how we are feeling than just text. We never listen to those that disagree with us but immediately shut them down.

While I agree that there is absolutely no use arguing with

someone on the Internet, I think we still need to be hyper aware to practice active listening in real life. We don't get the chance to do so in our main forms of communication these days, so when we get the chance, we need to take advantage of it. Especially when it comes to disagreements between our loved ones, friends, or co-workers. It helps us learn from one another and practice meaningful empathy. Perhaps practicing this so much is why actors are so empathetic and oftentimes labeled as over-dramatic or emotional?

I find myself wondering how much better the world would be if we listened more. Not just to the words that are said to us, but how they are said. What does body language tell us? Do people really mean those hateful remarks, or are they just scared? Also, more important than what they are saying is what they aren't saying. I don't know if I have any answers to these questions just yet, but I'm excited to continue my studies on this subject. I also recently discovered how easy it is to stop listening to yourself. A huge change in who I was took place, and I missed it because I wasn't paying attention.

I had a busy year. Work was taking off with huge projects. I was rehearsing, performing, and prepping for auditions all of my nights. I would easily have five-day strings of sixteen-hour days for months at a time. I had become a little too lost in my drive and work ethic. It's a trap that many of us fall into, especially those of us in huge metropolitan areas like New York City. Determined to keep going, I pushed through. I would check in with myself to make sure I was doing okay, but I wasn't actively listening. I was only checking to make sure I ate and showered, and that was about it.

Matt and I decided to redecorate our apartment, and while picking out items, I found myself constantly drifting toward gold pieces. Not like a yellowy goldenrod, but a more metallic, brass-like gold. This gold just looked so classy and sophisticated that I loved it! It definitely made me feel richer, more luxurious than I was. Than I ever had been. We eventually picked out a beautiful floor lamp, some coasters, and a large gold plate for our coffee table.

A little later on, I found myself drawn to even more gold things. After my ten-year-old laptop bit the dust, I made sure my new upgrade was the gold version, not the silver. I wanted a gold necklace, a gold notebook, even clothes that went well with gold. This was so unlike me, but it took me a while to notice. Gold was now my favorite color. A new favorite color that I didn't know I had. As vapid as it may sound, this sent me into a bit of an identity crisis.

Up until this point in my life, my favorite color had been orange. Not a reddish blood orange or a disgusting burnt orange. MY orange was the gauche, bright, not-quite-neon orange. My Texans would call this "Whataburger Orange." This was my favorite color. My color obsession.

I still remember the look of horror on my mother's face when I begged for a pair of bright orange Converse high tops in high school for my birthday. Even though she despised my color choice, she still sought them out and surprised me with them. These shoes would match my many orange shirts, room decorations, and of course, my collection of the aforementioned Whataburger order-number placards.

But somewhere along the way, orange had phased out of my life. Gone were the shoes and traces of orange decor or accessories. I had no idea when it happened, but orange was no longer my favorite color. I had given up a childish brashness for a more mature and elegant wash. I had to accept that gold was where my new allegiance lied, but I couldn't help but wonder how I missed the shift when it took place.

I hadn't taken the time to deeply listen to myself in a while. To really check in and see what was up. What I needed, what I still wanted, and more importantly, what I no longer wanted. Worst of all, I thought I had quashed this habit when I was younger. When I realized that if I had listened to myself, I would have discovered that I was gay long before I had to wrestle with myself to admit it. I was falling down on the job of taking the utmost care of myself, but luckily, this color war woke me up to the fact that I could do a better job listening to myself.

I'll never know what else I missed during the time my ears were plugged, but I do know that I'm going to try my hardest to not let it happen again. I hope you'll do the same. It's so incredibly difficult in this modern world of ours. We are more efficient than ever. We have more comforts and luxuries that keep our lives easy and keep us moving. In all of that moving, I implore you to find the time to talk to yourself. Have that meaningful conversation and find out what has changed. What is currently changing. If listening is so important to acting, how we strive to recreate believable moments, then it must be even more important in real life.

KEEP EXPLORING

WELL INTO MY first bout with unemployment, which was self-induced, mind you (oops), I was like, "Wow, I am really running low on money. Let's see if I can get my old job back." I was really, really smart, as you can tell, so I just picked up my phone and called good ol' Junior's to ask if I could come back and work. Well, the manager there said I would have to go in next Monday to file some new paperwork or whatever, but that I could, indeed, have my serving job back! Hooray!

I had foolishly quit the job, to "focus on auditioning" for the spring. My very first spring audition season in the city! NEVER DO THIS! Learn from my mistake for the love of everything holy, please! If you are thinking of quitting a job and jumping into something unknown, I'm here to tell you to keep that job a little bit longer while you slowly build your side hustle. Get that boat a little closer to the dock before you jump ship. You'll be much better off and much, MUCH less stressed, I promise you.

The Friday before I was set to return to waiting tables,

I received a final callback for a real live theatre show! I was a new, young, and eager actor, dying for the chance to perform in ANYTHING, and here was a non-union, off-off-off Broadway show offering a whole STIPEND and wanting me for a final callback round! I believe the stipend was around one thousand whole dollars for three weeks of rehearsal and two weeks of shows, which totaled out to about seven dollars per hour. A quarter under the minimum wage in New York City in 2013.

I was completely elated but at a loss for what to do, because unfortunately, the callback was scheduled for that next Monday, at the exact same time I was told to come in and file paperwork to renew my server status. I called the restaurant manager to ask if I could move the paperwork, like, an hour later, and he promptly told me, "If you aren't here when you said you would be, you don't have a job here!" Well, welcome to New York!

I, of course, did what any responsible young actor would do and said, "Screw him!" This callback was obviously my big break! So, I went. I sang well and read a few scenes, but immediately after, I was hit with the sad reality of being broke and not having a job at a time in America where jobs weren't that easy to find. Especially for someone right out of college in a brand new city. Oops again. Again, I do not recommend this route to anyone. Please be financially responsible because you will only harm yourself if you are not. So, I was still unemployed and desperately looking for a job. Then, by the grace of God Himself, I got the most miraculous phone call in the ramen aisle of a Washington Heights Rite Aid (a temple that now holds historic landmark status for its role in my life's journey).

I had spent the day traversing all over Manhattan, hawking myself to various Starbucks and Gap stores, desperate for any job. I even recruited my friend to my scheme and conned her into sweet-talking her manager at Starbucks for me. It would pay me eight dollars an hour for dreaded customer service, but hey, I was desperate. Seriously, people who work those jobs need to be paid more and treated way better. I'm a firm believer that you can tell everything you need to know about a person by how they treat the lowest rung of customer service associates. And though I won't name them, there are a few people I now aggressively avoid after I witnessed them berate some hardworking person doing their best to scrape by.

So there I was, standing in the middle of Rite Aid, looking very disheveled, mind you. I was about to spend my very last dollars on just enough instant ramen that, to my calculations, would give me one meal a day through the end of the week. I distinctly remember staring blankly into space while my friend did her best to cheer me up. She was talking about how wonderful it would be to work together and all the free coffee and food we could eat at Starbucks. Nutrition deficiency would be a thing of my past! Just as I was seeing a silver lining in my new reality, my phone rang.

No, it wasn't the show I had just auditioned for, but rather a casting director from an audition an entire six months prior, asking if I was free to be an immediate replacement in that show. Literally the craziest, most random phone call ever, but that's how it always happens, right? This offer was even better! It was a tour, it had a weekly salary attached, and best of all, it came with the Holy Grail: the Actors› Equity Card! "Oh to grace, how great a debtor, daily I'm constrained to be!"

After the offer, I didn't hear anything else come from the other end of the phone. In my pure shock, I just kept saying, "Yes, great, yes, okay, yes, sounds wonderful!" Once off the phone, we ditched the ramen, ran out of Rite Aid and hopped a train to the Times Square Red Lobster. Because when you book your first union-sanctioned actor job, you absolutely MUST celebrate with Cheddar Bay Biscuits!

The day after I accepted the offer, I went into the producers' office to sign the contract and pick up my script and score. Signing my first Actors' Equity contract meant I could join the union, which I did. I could now call myself a bonafide theatre professional, and best of all, I would no longer have to wait around for twelve hours without being seen at an audition. Plus, membership to the union meant my work would have salary minimums, pension, insurance, and even the fabled 401k. It was an increasingly rare catch for us millennials, and all but guaranteed to go extinct for Gen Z.

For this show, I would make about three hundred twenty dollars a week after taxes and union dues were taken out. Even though this was only a decade ago, I still had to look up how much money this would equal today, and Google tells me that it is the life-changing sum of three hundred fifty-seven dollars and fifty-three cents. This was more money than I had ever made in my entire life! I truly felt like a grown-up for a very, very short second when I signed that contract. And best of all, I was going to be performing for a living for the very first time. I would get an exhilaratingly refreshing respite from waiting tables or being screamed at by customers at some store. Thus began the first day of the rest of my life!

Honestly, how sad is it, that as actors, we are so desperate to get a job, any job, that we almost hardly care what the pay is? To this day, wages haven't gotten any better in the theatre world. We've recently seen a devastating devolution for funding of the arts. More than ever, organizations are struggling to cover all the costs it takes to produce theatre. Now, having sat on negotiating committees for Actors' Equity, I've seen first-hand how hard it can be for producing organizations to balance precariously thin budgets. Listen, y'all, theatre isn't necessarily a sustainable business model, but it is a necessary part of a community's culture. For children and adults, there are many proven benefits to attending and participating in live performances. It is essential for community and societal growth.

We now know that attending live theatre performances promotes deeper connections to our fellow humans, as well as to our own humanity in a way we cannot get in other forms of media. Theatre also helps us flex our empathy muscles when we witness storylines that go beyond our own life experiences. For children watching or participating, the performing arts builds imagination, relationship skills, collaboration skills, tolerance, and best of all, self-expression.

So, go out and support your local theater! Please go donate. Go buy tickets. Go buy a season subscription, even if you aren't going to be able to make it to every show. It truly means a lot to all of those artists involved, and you will make a huge difference in the lives of so many people. Many of these organizations even have educational programs that help troubled youth or any youth who desperately need a place in a community. We all had our "thing" that helped us through all of those awkward teenage years, and for myself and many, it was the theatre. Theatre is a place filled with empathy, love, and acceptance for those who might not quite fit in anywhere else.

The rehearsal period for this tour was unlike anything I will probably experience again. I was an immediate replacement for the lead actor in a children's musical called *Skippyjon Jones*. Based on the beloved children's book of the same name. The story follows a siamese cat named Skippyjon, who feels like he doesn't quite fit in with his family. He dreams of being a chihuahua superhero named El Skippito Friskito and goes on imaginary adventures in his safe space, which is quite literally, the closet.

Throughout his adventures, he would go on to save a chihuahua village from a big mean bumblebee who stole all of their frijoles. And with his newfound friends, Skippito would gain the courage to live his life as a chihuahua and even confess to his siamese cat mother that he identified as a chihuahua. After, of course, he returned to the real world by, well, coming out of the closet...

To actually see a story like this made for children was revolutionary to me. The score and songs were filled to the brim with Mexican flair. There was the flamenco palmas number or the climactic tango. There were Mexican guitars, maracas, and accordions backing us up. This celebration of my heritage was performed by an all-BIPOC cast. Performing for children who might not get to see these kinds of people or hear this kind of music often. I sure hope I shone brightly for the young Latine kids who were seeing themselves on stage for the first time. I sure hope I shone brightly for young Joshua.

Later, I would come to learn that the original lead actor had to leave the show because he had gotten himself arrested in some small town in, like, Kansas, I think? Kansas sounds right. But, I kid you not, somehow this guy, while touring the country as the lead in a children's musical, had some drunken altercation with a police officer or something and had gotten himself arrested. His loss, however, was my gain. But I digress.

In total, I had exactly four days of rehearsal. The day I signed the contract and picked up the script was included. I used that day to memorize the script and score as much as I could. I believe to this day that the pressure in this instance is why I still have incredibly fast memorization skills. I can completely memorize multiple pages of scenes in a matter of minutes, it's crazy. The next day would be in a rehearsal studio with an accompanist and the director. With them, I ran through all of the music, learning it... enough... and then ALL of the blocking and ALL of the choreography... enough.

On the third day, we focused on reviewing music for an hour, all-things costume and props the second hour, and then all blocking and choreography, until the stumble-through. In one of the greatest gifts I've ever been given, the director had brought his eight-year-old son to be his rehearsal assistant.

This kid LOVED the show and had seen it enough times that he basically knew it by heart, so he was my scene partner! For my stumble-through, it was just me playing my role and this eight-year-old playing every other role in the show with absolute commitment and abandon. I wasn't stressed or worried at all with him on stage with me. I remembered why I loved to do what I do. I remembered how to have fun, and, as they call it, play!

The next morning, after the exhausting whirlwind of rehearsals in New York City, I was pushed on an early morning flight and flown to meet the cast in Phoenix, Arizona. The stage manager on tour picked me up from the airport and drove me straight to the theater for my last day of rehearsal. I watched the cast perform the show twice before I even had the chance to meet them. After a quick lunch break, and a few quick ice-breaker questions between us, we immediately started my put-in rehearsal. This was my one and only chance to perform the show with the cast, lights, set, props, costumes, and music, and to everyone's surprise, it actually went well!

My debut performance would be the very next day. We wished the guy I was replacing well, and he flew back to New York City to deal with his business that morning. It was all so surreal and fast that, looking back, I think it was all exactly as it should have been. I mean, I would like to ask the producers, "WHAT THE HELL WAS EVERYONE THINKING!?" but I guess they somehow knew what they were doing.

From Phoenix, we traveled to Las Vegas then to Los Angeles and then all the way up the West Coast to Seattle.

Then we drove from there back to New York City, making stops at Salt Lake City, Denver, Mount Rushmore, and Ohio along the way. It was some of the most fun I've ever had, and I definitely recommend it to anyone at a young age. Older folks always say to make sure you do some traveling while you are young, and even though I still am young, I am going to go ahead and give it a strong "agree." Now is the time to do it!

And I can't think of a better way to travel and see our country than with six other barely-twenty-year-old actors, fresh out of college, all crammed into one van that also carried all of our set, costumes, equipment, and luggage. On a typical day, we would arrive at an elementary school's gymcafetorium, unload the entire van, put the whole set up ourselves, put the costumes in order ourselves, and go perform for all of these little children, most of whom had never even seen a live performance of anything before. It was work that truly filled my heart. After the show, usually two in a row, we would reverse course and be out of there by eleven in the morning, desperately needing a lot of food and a lot of strong coffee.

On certain special days, we would be invited to a meet-and-greet with some of the children after performances. Even while tired, probably dehydrated, and begging to get out of our hot costumes, it was worth every single moment to see the smiles on their faces. I mean, how often as a kid did you get to meet one of your favorite book characters?! You could see their eyes ignite with all of the wonder and amazement in the world, and it simply made my heart burst with joy. Looking at them, I often thought of kid Joshua. He would've died to see a live musical performance in his elementary school. How much he would have loved to ask for autographs or get his book signed by the character he'd read about so many times.

When you plan your life as an actor, you know your work is likely going to take you all over the place. I hadn't quite anticipated that I would get to explore my country less than a year after I graduated college, but hey, I'll take it! When we weren't in schools, we'd be at major theaters all around the West Coast. We'd perform anywhere from beautiful, modern, thousand-seat houses, to ancient stone Parthenons that were full of history. Thousands of performers had tread those boards, and we got to leave our stamp, too. In each new theater, I always made sure to walk as much of the space as possible, making my own exploration a "hello" of sorts to the space. Backstage, in the house, in the balconies, and even the lobbies. I wanted to know the space intimately, desperate for any Jedi-ghost-of-a-great-performer to pass on their knowledge to me.

After four long months and over a hundred performances, I returned to New York City unemployed, BUT as a new and proud member of Actors' Equity Association. With that Equity card in hand, there would be no more waiting in the freezing cold for hours and hours to then wait in the sweltering waiting room all day, just for a tiny chance to be seen at an audition. I had finally shoved my foot in the door, and the Man wasn't going to be able to shut it on me any longer. Well, at least not completely, anyway.

Strengthened from my expedition out West, I was prepared to compete with the pros! Ready to take the next steps in my career, whatever they would be. Once again, I was reminded of all I could accomplish if I gave it my all. I'm not quite sure what would have happened if I hadn't been able to learn the show so fast, but I think that kind of pressure is what drove me to success. There was no time to fail, or even to doubt success, in those few precious moments. Everyone was so supportive and never questioned if I would be able to pull it off. They all just believed I would, so I did, too. I guess we should always surround ourselves with those that believe in us. I really like the sound of that.

KEEP FAILING

How ABOUT WE play a game where we delve into all of the worst and most terrible audition fails that I have mostly brought upon myself up until this point in my life? Now, there are endless crazy stories on this subject, like the time my scene partner tried to hand me an unwrapped condom in the middle of our take, or the time a casting director nearly choked to death on her chicken caesar salad and left the room coughing while I was singing my face off for her. She didn't even have the consideration to cough on beat, I might add. But *these* fails are the ones that I brought upon myself.

Welcome to AUDITION FAILS:

1. My very first theatre open call audition in the city was for a pre-Broadway workshop of a new musical. In the room was the legendary casting director herself, Tara Rubin. Generally in the first phases of these open calls, you typically audition for the casting

intern or someone like that, but of COURSE, Tara Rubin was in the room to experience the steaming pile of shite that was my audition. I confidently walked into the room, ran over my tempo with my accompanist, and took my power stance in the middle of the room. Standing tall, with my legs shoulder-width apart. Eyes looking just over the head of the auditor, no direct eye contact. Arms... probably doing something awkward because what are you supposed to do with your arms when you sing? As the accompanist started to play the opening measures of music, it didn't sound familiar. Much to my dismay, as the music played, I couldn't hear where I was supposed to enter. The vamping piano was suddenly an indistinguishable wave of notes, and I could not for my life find where to jump in. I remember breaking the cardinal rule of NO DIRECT EYE CONTACT and blankly staring directly at Tara Rubin as if she were going to give me my cue. FACE. PALM. Finally, after what seemed like an agonizing five minutes of continuous vamping, I just started singing. While I was definitely wrong on my entrance, the brilliant accompanist quickly caught up with me and expertly followed throughout the rest of the audition. Of course, shaken from the disaster of the beginning of the audition, the rest wasn't much better. After the pianist hit the last chord, putting me out of my misery, I choked out a solemn "thank you." Tara so graciously thanked me, and then added the note, "Well, you know what you need to work on." With my face emblazoned red, I replied that I did, I will. I gathered my music and ran out of the room.

Fail Score: 8.5 out of 10 stars

There was no excuse for not knowing my music better and delivering a solid thirty-two-bar cut in an audition room. This is literally the bare minimum an actor is supposed to be able to do. Extra points for making a terrible first impression on a very important casting director. You better believe I've always made sure to study my music better and know exactly how it sounds with just a bare piano.

2. Number two is one of the only times I completely lost my nerve. I pride myself on almost never being nervous. I can go into the room calm, cool, collected, and ready to do my work. But when I was called back for one of my absolute dream roles on The Broadwáy, I unexpectedly choked so hard that I was shaken to my core for a little while. The role was Boq in *Wicked*. The munchkin boy who has his heart set on Glinda, and who later becomes known as The Tin Man. Also, for the record, this is still one of my dream roles, so if anyone can just let the esteemed casting directors at Telsey know, I would greatly appreciate it! I had been given a huge packet of material to prep the night before, a few songs, a few pages of all different scenes. This being my dream role, I, of course, already knew every word by heart and was absolutely confident that I would crush it. As I walked into the room,

the casting director said we'd do the two songs and then move on to the sides. Great! We began the session with a duet, and they had brought in an actress who had previously played the role of Nessarose on Broadway to read and sing with me. The problem with this plan was that she sang in the duet first. As soon as she started singing, I felt it. Her voice was so incredibly beautiful and perfect that in that single instant I felt like a fraud. I mean, I could never sound like that. As soon as that doubt set in, it radiated the heat of nervousness throughout my entire body. Sweaty palms, weak knees, mom's spaghetti. What was happening to me?! I'd heard of other performers occasionally dealing with this type of audition anxiety, but this didn't happen to *ME*. I fought so hard to keep focus, and after learning from big audition fail number one, I was still able to sing things correctly, albeit a bit wobbly. We moved on from the singing and to the sides, and things were still rocky, but for the most part on the track. I got the laughs, I didn't trip on a line. However, as I left, it was clear I wasn't moving forward in the process, and I was shaken up for a few weeks.

Fail Score: 5 out of 10 stars

This was still a solid fail, but mostly only due to the high stakes. From this, I learned I needed to practice viewing those "big auditions" the exact same as the less life-changing ones. It's a practice that I'm still perfecting but have gotten much better at. I no longer put myself under all of that unnecessary pressure, because at the end of the day, it's just a gig. No one I love is going to die or love me less because I screwed it up.

3. For musicals, there are dance auditions or dance calls. For performers who have trained hardcore in dance and are really good, these are their primary bread and butter. We call this amazing class of athletes "Dancer Dancers." There is a level below the powerhouse Dancer Dancer for those of us who have taken many dance classes but don't keep up with training rigorously, don't have the flexibility to kick our face, or the size and strength to throw a girl in the air. This middle class in the theatre world is known as "Movers." I am a proud Mover. Note: There is technically an even lower class than Movers for the truly uncoordinated, but as a courtesy, we just lump them in with the Movers, give them a little extra encouragement, and put them in the back. Bless their hearts. Now, once upon a time, there was a big regional production of the musical *Oliver!* at a very prestigious regional theatre. I had gone to audition, and when asked about my dancer "class," I replied that I was a Mover. Casting loved that for me and sent me to the invited dance call. Typically, the invited dance call is for the movers and we learn a combo that is dumbed down to middle-class level, and everyone has a grand ole time. Well, this was in the *Newsies* heyday, and every single musical wanted

extreme acrobatic/gymnastic dancing, and by GOD if this production of *Newsies*, I mean *Oliver!*, wasn't going to have it. Halfway into sweatily trying to learn the combo, I started debating whether I should just walk out. There were double pirouettes, Russians, torres, fouettés, macarons, Chanels, and many other French words I couldn't make out, all in this eight-count combo. I stayed and tried to power through. During the parts where I didn't know what to do, I put on a big smile and gestured to my Dancer Dancer neighbor a la Vanna White to present him executing a perfect leap with multiple rotations. I was, unsurprisingly, cut during the first round, and I have never been happier to leave an audition.

Fail Score: 3 out of 10 stars

Honestly, I probably shouldn't have given into defeat as much as I did during this call. However, I refuse to take most of this one on, because how was I supposed to know I would need to be in peak gymnast shape to be in *OLIVER!*? I mean, did Fagan's boys really need to be tumbling across the stage during "You've Got to Pick a Pocket or Two"? They did me dirty.

4. Now, self-tapes have become the norm these days. To be a successful actor, you simply have to learn the science of making a good self-tape. You must make sure you have the audio capabilities and software know-how to pull off a singing self-tape. You need to

know how to produce a video where you can be seen, heard, have the accompaniment. It's a huge technical shift of what was expected of your average actor, even just within the last decade. One time, I had submitted for a role in a musical on a cruise ship. I was set to leave town for the week of auditions, but I still submitted anyway, in case they asked me for a self-tape. Well, they did, but not until late the day before I was leaving town. Bummer. All of my equipment was in my New York apartment, so I was going to have to film it before I left so I could get it in on time. In the worst decision ever, I decided that I would learn all of the material that night, and then wake up super early in the morning to film it before I had to leave. Yes, you heard that right. I thought it would be a wise idea to have only ONE whole hour at seven in the morning to film myself singing a super high, belty musical theatre number. As you can imagine, voices aren't so good first thing in the morning and usually land an octave lower. I tried to warm it up, desperately prepping for a good take, but it was all in vain. The footage was a struggle! I sounded like a poor boy going through puberty with absolutely no control over my voice. Though a little strained, I eked out my best take and sent it in, figuring I couldn't say no. I've never heard from this casting office ever again. EVER AGAIN.

Fail Score: 9 out of 10 stars

This one was very bad. The only driving force in this situation was me. At every point along the way, I had the chance to stop it. I could've said NO at any point, but for some reason I felt like I couldn't. I felt like I had to send in a tape, no matter what. And obviously filming in the morning was a mistake I'll never make again. Oof, apologies to whomever had to watch that tape.

5. The summer after my junior year of college, I was off in New York City training and preparing to eventually move there the next summer after graduation. Back home in Texas, a regional theatre I knew and loved was auditioning for a production of *Spring Awakening*. This production was slated to be one of the very first regional productions of the show in the country, and everyone I knew was excited to audition for it! I was a bit bummed that I would have to miss the audition, but I just figured I wouldn't be there, so I couldn't possibly be considered. I heard from friends that the auditions and callbacks went well, but that director still wanted to audition more guys to fill out the cast. That was crazy. In the back of my mind, I kept wondering if I should email the director and ask to be considered, but I felt so insignificant, and I didn't want to be annoying. I had no idea when they planned to hold those new auditions, and I still wouldn't even be back in Texas for a whole week-and-a-half! At that point, I went to the head instructor of the training program I was attending

and asked her what she thought I should do in that situation. When I asked her, I felt so stupid. I had obviously missed the audition. It was what it was… Then she looked me directly in the eye and asked me, "What the hell is wrong with you?!" followed by, "You sit down right now and write an email with your headshot and resume, explain that you are in New York City receiving top-notch training, and that you'd love to be considered when you are back." She forced me to write out the email, right then and there. After a quick double-check from her, I sent it. A week before I was due to leave New York City, I got an email from the theatre that said they would love to have me audition. I flew in on a Thursday, that Friday was spent frantically learning songs from the show, Saturday I went in and sang a few songs, including the Ernst part in "Touch Me," and finally Sunday was the callback audition with all of the guys. It was a whirlwind of a weekend that almost never happened because I didn't believe that I was worth considering. Later the next week, I was all alone in my apartment in Waco, Texas one afternoon, when the theatre called to offer me the role of Ernst. I struggled to hold in the joyful screams until I hung up. *Spring Awakening* would be my first professional show. I would make a two-hour drive between Waco and Dallas for two months to perform in the show, while simultaneously attending the first semester of my senior year. Plus, I got to play the romantic inter-est opposite my future husband, Matt, who had been cast as Hanschen. Fun fact: the director had no idea that we were a couple when he cast us. We hadn't even read a scene together during the callback process. But the universe worked extra hard to make this one happen for sure!

Fail Score: 2 out of 10 stars

Okay, I know you may be surprised that I consider this a fail. In a lot of ways, I won. I mean, I did book it! But I still can't get over the fact that I almost let such a golden opportunity slip through my fingers. I didn't feel like I had enough value, or authority, or whatever to simply ask to be considered for this show. I didn't have anything to lose. I wouldn't have made a bad impression if they weren't able to accommodate me for an audition, or even if they weren't interested. The absolute worst thing that could have happened was if the theatre politely declined. From that point on, I never questioned anything like this again. The worst anyone can do is say no. As long as you are polite and don't press the issue, there is never any harm in asking. Go after something that you really want.

6. As Netflix started pumping out original content, one show caught my attention right off the bat. *Unbreakable Kimmy Schmidt* was everything I had hoped for in a television show. A quirky character comedy created by my idol, Tina Fey. This show was so quick, unrelentingly hilarious, and filled to the brim with character actors. Actors who were different and celebrated for

being so. And it was cast and filmed out of New York City! I just knew that if I were to get my start in the television character actor scene that it would be with this show. During casting for the first season, I was called into the casting office for a small, no-line role. The office was incredibly warm, which made all nerves disappear. And while I didn't book the role, I clearly made an impression on that office. Over the course of the four seasons, I would be called in for three more roles, and even called back for a larger, recurring role. I knew I was perfect for this show, and casting felt like I was a great fit every time. I knocked each audition out of the park. I was fully memorized, prepared, gave choices with each take, took notes, made the auditors laugh and smile, and most of all, had fun. Each one of these roles weren't in the cards for me. Each one passed me by. While it was a knife through the heart, I knew I was making progress and that it would just be a matter of time until I could be a part of this show. When it was finally announced that the show would conclude with a longer movie-like special episode, my heart sank. I only had one more chance. Shockingly, I was called in for a role in this final episode. Again, my audition rocked! I got to see my casting friends again and play in this world that I so very much wanted to live in, at least for a little while. But a few days later, I realized I didn't book that role either. I was devastated. I did everything I could. I did everything "right". I never gave up. And yet I would never be in the *Unbreakable Kimmy Schmidt* family. That had been the very last chance, and it didn't happen for me.

Fail Score: 0 out of 10 stars

Despite my best efforts, this was still a huge failure. It's even one of the most painful, as there was nothing I could have done differently. I gave everything I had, so many times, and I was still let down. But I don't take any blame upon myself. Sometimes that's just the way life works out, isn't it?

All right, so the total score from all of these fails is:

27.5 / 60 stars. Remember, we're playing golf rules here, so the lower the better. I did just a bit better than the halfway point. Not the best, but I'll take it.

But you didn't expect me to do well in a chapter about failing did you?

Thank you for playing this game with me. I hope you had a lot of fun. And I do sincerely hope that you will join me next time with a few of your own! Feel free to share with me at @joshwadam on Instagram. All confidentiality will be maintained!

KEEP LOVING

THE THING THAT I'm probably most proud of in the entire world is my marriage. I got married incredibly young. Well, incredibly young for my generation, a New Yorker, and a gay man. Statistically, I shouldn't even have gotten married at all, but I did!

I would have been a fool to let such a gorgeous soul pass through my life without at least attempting to lock him down for forever. I know all spouses rhapsodize about their significant other, but I am seriously astonished everyday by Matt. He's incredibly patient and easy going, and yet he simultaneously possesses a work ethic and determination to match an Olympian.

He is always the best at anything he picks up. Swimming, photography, web design, play development, project management, marketing, brand development, content creation. It's SO annoying. Over the years, I've quite enjoyed watching his bosses marvel in amazement at all he can do. I've loved cheering him on as he started a new career out of nowhere, and within a year, rocketed through the ranks of his company.

In 2019, after years in the theatre world, he left his job managing Broadway shows to jump to the multimedia marketing agency VaynerMedia, the company created and helmed by social media mogul Gary Vaynerchuk. And how did he land his job there? Well, he simply emailed Gary himself! A perfect pitch of his skills, an understanding of Gary's processes, and the gumption needed to prove himself. And I knew he would be successful. After all, this is MY HUSBAND!

People always ask, "Why did you get married so young? Are you sure?" And while I want to pterodactyls cream in their face or ask them why they knowingly spend money at Dunkin' Donuts (ew), instead I grin, nod, and say something like, "Oh, when you know, you'll understand." It's usually mysterious enough for them to actually believe it and let me off the hook.

But then I realize how true that statement was for me. I definitely don't think that it happens like that for everyone, and I consider myself incredibly fortunate. But, I did just *know*. Within my actual being, down beyond the deep tissue and my bones, and into someplace that I didn't know existed. I *knew*. And when Matt brought up the idea of getting married, I activated my trap card, and I locked him down as fast as I could.

My favorite part of marriage is the challenge. Sure, the cuddles, the company, and getting to spend so much time with my best friend is great, too, but if you've learned anything about me in this book, it's that I love a challenge. The fun of life is overcoming them, and it's how we continue to better ourselves. I'm not too interested in a life where I stay stagnant.

Marriage is HARD work. It's especially tough with two ambitious, driven people like the two of us. It helps that we both have similar backgrounds and our fundamental values are in place together. But, a life in the arts comes with a lot of unknowns and time apart. At one point, we had to seriously consider moving far away from the city. Matt was up for an associate artistic director position at a prominent regional theatre. A path he had been pursuing for some time, but it just didn't make the cut for us at the time. Moving away from New York City is something that I don't think I could ever do, for now at least, but I know it's something that Matt still sometimes thinks about.

Through all of it, though, we know that we are wholly committed to solving all the problems together. I think that is the difference between a marriage that works and one that doesn't. A good, strong marriage doesn't mean that you'll never fight or disagree, but that hopefully your disagree-ments won't necessarily look like fights. At the end of the day, you are committed to taking the time to sort them out, not giving up and throwing in the towel.

Matt and I both come from homes of divorce, and we've seen tons of bad examples of what a marriage could be. In my opinion, our parents' generation, the full generation before us, had a very strong sense of entitlement with a side of selfishness. We saw these baby boomers regularly display the traits that have now made them infamous. At least the folks that we were around. Once that selfishness spread to the marriage, we saw couples refuse to work together. They had too much pride. They always had to be right. They possessed the entitlement that they were "owed" whatever they wanted, when they wanted it. All of these traits would rip any marriage apart.

Since we vowed to not let that become us, we had to discover very quickly what works and what doesn't in our own marriage. The main thing we found, and I cannot stress this enough, is COMMUNICATION. I know everyone says that, but it's hard to really know what that means. We've found we need healthy debates with one another. Never yelling, never trying to hurt the other's feelings. If we are upset and can't debate or talk it out at the moment, then we wait until we can. Think of marriage as one big, long conversation.

Most of all, NEVER have a fight over text messages or on the phone. Always in-person. We made this mistake early on in our relationship. I had been out for a night drinking with friends… Matt didn't understand why I still was out so late. Tipsy, I couldn't quite communicate well over text. He couldn't read my tone. And a simple little thing turned into a blow out.

Take your time to really think about how you are feeling and describe it to your partner. Describe exactly how you feel, and more importantly WHY. It doesn't have to make sense or be rational. For example, if I forget to throw away a piece of trash or put up a dish I used, Matt gets very upset. The way his brain and emotions process that action is that I don't care about our household. That I don't care to respect the house and home that we have built together, which leads him to believe that I don't care about him.

It doesn't matter if I agree or disagree that he should feel that way. The fact of the matter is that is how he feels. Just one dish. Since I don't want to upset him, I try my very best to make sure everything is clean, put away, and thrown away. In return, he gives me as much grace as he can when I forget. And I forget all the time. He understands that I'm not wired to believe that a single dish represents an urge to disrespect him, but it's just a manifestation of my type-B scatterbrain. As long as he sees me trying and doing better, he gives me the grace to not be perfect.

You have to take care of all the mundane squabbles. Really understand where each other is coming from. The little squabbles and disagreements are the most dangerous. Everyone has them, and not dealing with them will let them collect and build into a great chasm between you. Before you know it, it's too big to fix. A couple of times, especially early in our relationship, we probably got a little closer to that happening than we would've liked. We were lucky enough to identify it quickly. We sat down as adults and talked about what all was bothering us. We communicated clearly to get through it. And at the end of the day, people who are fighting don't want to have sex, so if you wanna get laid, you better keep it all peaceful and fruitful, okay?

Oddly enough, we learned how to communicate well with each other through working together on big projects very early in our relationship. Whether we knew it or not, being able to work together on something was so inherent to what we were both looking for in a partner. And now it all makes sense, as a marriage is simply two people working to build a life together.

We hear all the time from couples that they don't think they would be a good working partner for their significant other. Honestly, I don't understand how people have marriages where they don't think that they could work with their spouse. If you feel like you cannot work with them, how is this partnership going to be a successful one?

Marriage is all about working together to solve problems. Arguably bigger and more important ones than one could ever encounter in your line of work. You have to work together to establish a stable household, physically and financially. If kids are involved, there are challenges to conquer together every day. If you don't think you could work with someone, why get married and try to work at the job of life with them every day?

While we were both attending college, we were approaching a summer where neither of us had anything lined up. Being driven, we knew that we wanted to do something ambitious and creative to give us a jumpstart on our careers. So, we decided to see if we could produce our own summer show. It would be our own summer musical that we would put up on our college campus, not wasting those resources we were paying top dollar for.

If there are any students, or soon-to-be college students, reading this, I cannot express enough how MANY resources you have at your fingertips. Please realize that you will likely not have this kind of easy, "free" access to these resources again ever in your life. I implore you to use them as much as you can while you are there. You are paying a hefty penny for that tuition, and it would be a shame to not use every single thing that that money is paying for. Every single student should be coming out of college with a stellar, complete portfolio: ALL the pictures, video, websites, and content of your work that you could ever dream of! There are students in the communication and media departments in your universities that will be more than happy to help you set these things up. They're also wanting to get that experience and portfolio, so use this and reach out to them if you need any help.

We took this approach when we decided to produce our own show. We found a small-cast, new musical called *Dani Girl*. This hilarious musical was about two children who are fighting through cancer, and the majority of it takes place in their hospital room, but also in their imaginary adventures to find out "Why Cancer Is."

Incredibly beautiful, this show was written by Michael Kooman and Christopher Dimond, two musical theater writers who have had very successful careers writing for Disney's *Vampirina* and a myriad of other successful projects. Somehow, Matt had convinced them to give us the rights to do their show as a summer project, so we ran with it.

The next person we had to convince was the head of the theatre department. My nemesis. This particular man is still one of the most toxic people I have ever encountered in my life. He had some weird belief that students should not be involved in any outside professional work while they were students. Even during the summers. I think he was afraid that they would start their careers early and leave the school, and the department would lose money maybe? Who knows, but it ended up causing huge fights between him and me after I would get cast in not one, but two outside shows while still in college.

All we would need for *Dani Girl* would be the space,

which would be empty anyway, and utilities. We showed our proposed budget, all the funds we would raise ourselves, and we showed him how we would be giving more opportunities to students right there on campus. We would need a stage manager, other performers, a costume designer, lighting designer, scenic designer, director, and music director. Tons of positions! He gave his blessing, probably thinking it would be a lot smaller than it ended up being, and we were off to the races. We brought all of the students on board, scraped together this production, and to our surprise, it was kind of life-changing, especially in our professional lives.

During the process, our small, little-show-that-could received so much good press and local notoriety for the level of professionalism that we pulled off. In Matt's beginnings of a great marketer, he made sure to get us in as many publications as possible. We were in all of the local papers, magazines, and even performed a number on the local radio station. We were even reviewed by the most revered critic in town! Our audiences and critics understood how much people needed a show like this to talk about a very hard issue.

Those two months were very, very hard. We were organizing and working with people who were still in college and didn't necessarily have the same work ethic or standards that we had at that time. We were all trying to figure out how to be professional and work at the top of our game and craft, things that are triple-challenging at that age. Matt and I were the heads of our own theatre company in the blink of an eye. We had to make big budgetary decisions and personnel decisions that are usually reserved for artistic directors at established theaters.

This process really cemented a relationship between us as we learned, not only how to work together, but the conflict resolution that is needed to focus on a project and get results. We also learned that we absolutely *love* working with each other. We both understand the way the other›s mind works. We know our weaknesses and strengths. We naturally fell into a rhythm of dividing the work in correlation to which one of us loves it.

Ultimately, I learned that I didn't really love the producer role, or at least the managing director role, where I was placed. Matt really found his voice as the leader, and I loved watching that happen for him. I loved being by his side and working with him to create something so beautiful. In a way, I guess *Dani Girl* was our first child. We put so much blood, sweat, and tears into the project that the returns were tenfold. Once we got that first high from that hit, it ignited a pattern of us working together on various projects. Leading, hopefully, to us working together one day soon to build our own family.

Our production of *Dani Girl* went on to be a selection in a new works theatre festival in Dallas that attracted a lot of big-name artists in the region. It gave both of us our first introduction to the professional theatre world in Dallas. Which, by the way, is an amazing theatre scene. From there, we worked in Dallas a few times while we were still in college. Being in those professional shows and getting that experience never would've happened if we hadn't gone all-in and really put in that effort to create our own work.

Everything in this world is about execution, how much you are willing to work at something, and how many sacrifices you are willing to put in to get what you want. Whether that be a fulfilling marriage or the next step in your career, nothing worthwhile is ever handed to you on a silver platter. And I know, as very few things have been handed to me on a silver platter, same for my husband. I wish more people would really realize this. I want them to really go after what they want because they deserve it. We all do. We all deserve to meet our goals and to see our work reach its true potential!

It wasn't until a few years later after we had established ourselves at least a little bit in New York City that we came out to our parents. Initially, both sets of conservative Texan parents did not approve, but, I am glad to say, through a lot of laughing and killing them with kindness, they have all really come around. It was a little scary since they were all very conservative Texas Christian folks. Due to their location and upbringing, none of them had ever really seen openly gay people before, let alone have any type of relationship with a member of the LGBTQ+ community.

I always thought I would regret coming out to my parents as late as I did, but I don't. I think it is important, no matter who you are, to come out whenever you're ready to whomever you are ready to tell. And those are very personal choices. Also, the way in which you come out is only your choice, and nobody should have a criticism of it or a judgment about it.

As I was telling my mother, I remember her demanding I tell her why I hadn't told her sooner. She made it all about her and how it made her feel; I was just so angry about her selfishness. Angry that she couldn't see that it's not about her. At all. As much as it does affect our relationship, at the end of the day, it's only about me, and I guess Matt, too. But it's definitely not about her. When it comes to my family, I try to lead with as much grace as possible. While I don't excuse any bad behavior, I understand the religious conservative culture they have been steeped in for their entire lives.

My parents took a lot longer to get on our side than Matt's did. Regretfully, neither one of my parents attended our wedding, a fact that is still particularly hurtful to this day. They weren't clear what their plans were. I do think my father, ever a poor communicator, tried to tell me he wasn't going to come the day before. My mother was even more cryptic about her situation. So I didn't really know they weren't going to be there until the day of. And even then, I couldn't have been one hundred percent sure until I walked in to see all of my beautiful friends and family. But not them.

An unexpected wave of relief washed over me. I wouldn't have to try to tiptoe around them that night. I was able to really be myself. After all, I had just invited them as a courtesy, even though I didn't quite realize it until that moment. I had my chosen family with me. Some were blood, most were not, but my family was with me that night.

Their actions did cause a little bit of an estrangement and a giant strain on my relationship with both of them. I don't necessarily feel bound to them as family, but I do still love them. It's taken multiple years to remember to choose love over anything and to keep on loving them and forcing them to come around if they want me in their lives. Forcing them to accept that Matt is more important to me than they are. Luckily, I have seen a great change in both of them. My mom, at least, may love Matt more than me and asks about him every time we speak. It makes my heart smile to see them finally starting to come around.

Of course, my brothers and their wives had probably always known I was gay since I was five years old. They gave me a little flack for waiting so long to tell them, but they have always been more than supportive and loving in everything that I do. They all attended our wedding and even had a blast on the dance floor with all of our theatre friends. I think I may have learned how to choose love from them more than anyone. I really am so thankful for them. They have also played a huge role in helping my parents see the love between Matt and me. That maybe their minds were a little too closed. At the end of the day, love is love, and we can only wish for more of it in the world.

KEEP REMINDING

This lovely haiku goes out to all those writers, creators, and casting directors out there.

Not all Latinos
Are on the streets or deal drugs,
So kindly, FUCK OFF!

Very much yours truly,

Joshua Gonzales

KEEP HUSTLING

As AN ACTOR, I've too long subscribed to the false line of thinking that we MUST have a super flexible work schedule that allows us to be available for auditions and work at all times. While I understand how that *idea* makes sense, it often doesn't actually come to fruition how we think it will. In pursuit of the perfectly flexible job, we often find ourselves in low-level customer service jobs. Due to the low paying nature of these jobs, we actually find ourselves taking on several of them just to make ends meet. Working long hours, getting yelled at by customers, all to still lack the funds to pay for headshots or the energy to wake up at six in the morning for that audition.

I think I now subscribe to having a more permanent, well-paying, full-time job. One that allows the security that keeps your stress low and energy high, while also providing the funds to pay for the expenses you need for your passion hustles. I think this can apply to all areas of passion, not just acting. If you make yourself invaluable to a position, odds are that your employer will work with you to take the time off when you need to for a project. Or you'll find yourself taking on projects that actually pay you and treat you right, because those are the only ones worth losing your day job over.

A selection of jobs I have held before quitting, getting fired, or booking work that made me leave include: waiting tables at Junior's in Times Square, selling bite-sized cupcakes to people from nine in the morning to ten at night, running a cash grab booth in the middle of Grand Central Station, filing donation paperwork for a homelessness charity, being a weekend doorman for a building in midtown Manhattan, programing the entire class offerings for an actor training facility, handing out jackets to New York City Marathon runners, and two grueling days slinging coffee in the cafe at the Upper East Side Barnes & Noble.

My favorite, and probably *the* craziest job I ever had was as a Cluemaster at one of the first escape room establishments in the country. This was before the escape room craze really caught on, so this sounded like the most bonkers place to work. Of course I wanted the job! Now, they are very popular all around the world, but if you haven't heard, the premise is simple: you and your friends are locked in a room for an hour, and you have to try to escape. There are clues, locks, and different puzzles that you have to decipher in order to ultimately escape the room, sans brute force.

I'm not even completely sure how I landed it. I'm sure I was fresh off of a gig, unemployed, and sent my resume to everyone that I could. All I know is that I interviewed, and they wanted me. As a Cluemaster, I would lead people through a short introduction about how the game worked. I would wish them luck, lock the door, and then go watch them from a centralized control room with all my Cluemaster buddies, occasionally giving my imprisoned group a hint to further their quest to, well, escape the room. It even paid above minimum wage at eleven dollars per hour.

It was fun and not much real work, but what really made the job was the atmosphere and the wonderful people I met who became my lifelong friends. We were ALL actors. It was the coolest to get to sit around all day with people who understand what you are going through. We were astoundingly, completely supportive of one another in our jobs and careers. Last-minute covers for auditions, well wishes for jobs, and the farewell parties for the ones who left us to go on to much better things than sitting around for hours in our little hovel of a control room. We were a family. And we shared some insane experiences at that place, just like any family would.

One of my favorite moments happened on my very first time cluemastering solo. I had just completed my training and was working on a game by myself for the first time. Next to me, huddled over the single table in the control room, were two people that I had never met. Fellow Cluemasters. One of them was Ken, and I knew right away that we would be good friends.

Ken is what happens when you mix two-parts Chris Farley, one-part Pauly D, and sprinkle in a touch of the genuine pureness of Tom Hanks. I was immediately drawn to his wit. He's lightning-fast in finding the funny in everything and would go any distance for a laugh. Using his erratic, boundless energy to shock those around him in amazement, sometimes so loud that players locked in the rooms could hear him. And yet, instead of being a douchey ass like so many of these types of comedians are, Ken has the most loyal and earnest soul of anyone I've met. He's genuinely happy for all his friends' successes, and is always a huge supporter of me in whatever I do. Good people.

Ken was running the first game that fateful morning. I was watching and trying to learn his style of cluemastering. Suddenly, a player in his room started pacing around next to the door. This was a little odd, as the rest of the group was hard at work, trying to solve the puzzle. Ken figured the player was bored of the game and just wanted to hang back.

Then it happened. The player's breakfast made an appearance all over the floor of the room where he was trapped... with his family and three strangers. From the looks of the giant puddle of puke, last night's dinner was also invited to the party. I've honestly never seen that much vomit in my life. It covered half of the floor of the room in about a half-inch layer. Thick like frosting.

Of course, my new coworker Ken rushed in immediately to clear the room and attend to the man, who was magically cured after his demons had been expelled. But then, there I am. Brand-new, not knowing what I can do to help my new coworkers clean up a monster-sized pile of bile. I was terrified that this is what the job really was.

After the group left, Ken grabbed a mop bucket, gloves, and a roll of paper towels. This poor guy then got down and started scooping up the sludge until there was little enough that it could be mopped up. I could not believe it! He gained immense respect from me for that, as I would have just quit and left. I needed a job, but I was not about to scoop up another man's bits 'n' chunks for eleven dollars an hour. But I will say that I will never forget that moment. Or the two people I shared it with. Nothing will bond people faster than a lake of grown-man spew.

I could honestly write this entire book just about experiences like that and the countless things I saw while working these games a million times. Work enough games and you'll see it all. You see every possible way people can misinterpret clues, how many times they will not find the thing in plain sight, and you will be flashed multiple times. It happens. But what is remarkable is what it taught me about people and relationships.

You can learn a whole lot watching people play with their families, strangers, or significant others. Everyone has unique characteristics that taught me so many invaluable nuances about the human experience. I studied these people and strove to replicate them in my work. What baffled me the most was the social misogyny that I witnessed every day. There was always a woman who would be right or want to try to solve something, and her man would not listen to her, would straight-up tell her she was wrong, or simply wouldn't let her try. Without even realizing it (or sometimes on purpose), people would act in the most overtly racist and classist ways. It was incredible to bear witness to humanity in such an unlikely place.

While our games would run, my coworkers and I would hustle for our acting careers. We would learn monologues, work scenes with each other, and of course, scroll through the breakdowns. The breakdowns are essentially the job ads for actors. Casting directors post a project they are casting and list the descriptions of the roles. You either submit for a particular role you fit and hope they call you in for an audition, or the job is an open call and you show up for that particular audition.

One night while working the late games, I saw a breakdown for a hidden-camera television show on ABC. It's rare that major network projects of any kind are in the public breakdowns, since typically casting directors only send the big projects to agents. So you have to have an agent submit you. I immediately thought that this could be my chance to get a foot in the door at ABC.

Casting was looking for a person over eighteen to play a teenage boy, preferably someone of an ethnicity, who had lots of improv experience. This breakdown was written for me, so I immediately submitted myself, making sure to include a note about my years of improv experience. I mean, how could they say no? I spent four years in the very campus-famous improv troupe at my college. It was basically SNL-level training, right?!

They must have thought so, as I soon had an audition for that next Tuesday. I headed to the ABC building on the Upper West Side and walked into a swank office waiting room. The audition would take place with the producers inside the most gorgeous conference room. Two producers of the segment took two of us into the room and explained a little scenario. He told us that we were two friends hanging out, and I was to help the other guy come out of the closet.

I was like, great, sounds good to me! And we both went

back-and-forth improvising a whole dramatic scene. I tried to encourage him to come out of the closet, and he didn't want to because he was afraid. At one point, we were both crying, and the producers were eating it up. I could tell everyone was surprised at how real it got in that moment. And the next day, I received an offer.

That phone call was when I found out that the segment would be for the hit show *What Would You Do?* with John Quiñones. The filmed segment would be a little different from the audition. This segment was about two teenage boys who would be FORCING another boy to come out of the closet while at lunch at a diner. The hope was that all of the innocent patrons eating next to these boys would chime in or say something to get these bullies off of his back.

The next week, we met the production team at the headquarters, and they shuttled us to a diner in New Jersey where we would film for the day. And of course, I remember having to ask for coverage for my shift for the day of filming because I was scheduled to work. I had to beg and explain to them that this was a big gig for national television. I was able to find a friend to cover, so I lucked out a bit. Thank you, Arielle.

When we arrived at the diner, we took a tour and got to know the space. The crew had already decked out the place with hidden cameras and microphones everywhere. We would know where the crew would sit and watch and where the "marks" would sit. As we started getting our directives, I suddenly became really nervous.

I would be interacting with a lot of strangers, pressing them in a fictitious situation that could get pretty tense. They were unknowing participants in our little experiment. But, I

132 | Joshua Gonzales

knew the good that this could bring into the world. I knew that a segment like this could spark conversations in homes that desperately needed them. Conversations that would be helpful for the world, and especially for LGBTQ+ people. If I could further the cause with my profession, I would do it. Full out, no marking.

The producers gave us earpieces to stay in constant communication with us. At times, they spoke in our ears and even told us what to say next. Maneuvering the conversations around what would help the segment, while also avoiding any big blow ups. The show is one hundred percent real. I KNOW that there are reality shows that are heavily scripted, or very much pushed in a deliberate way, but it was a breath of fresh air to know that this show was still one hundred percent real. Everyone who got involved with us and told me off for being a bully was a genuine real person, and those were their real feelings.

There was the woman who was so moved that she actually walked over and comforted the boy we were bullying. And her mother, who chastised me, and the third for being so pushy with him. Though a few refused to get involved, I was so stunned to see even older straight men butting in, in defense of someone and an identity they knew little about. Even if they may not be onboard with the LGBTQ+ community, they still understood the negative impact the bullying could have on another human. And perhaps the most moving was the brand-new mother, with her infant right beside her, who broke down and screamed at us for what we were doing. She was desperate to make the world a better place for her brand-new daughter.

The thing I loved most, though, was that the producers understood that this was a sensitive topic. They knew that as LGBTQ+ actors ourselves, it was meaningful for all of us to get it right. They respected our wishes to make sure the people that we encountered wouldn't leave upset. So, after every single scene, after they revealed to the unknowing participants that this was a hidden-camera show, they would let all three of us have a little chat with them.

We were able to apologize for tricking them, and more importantly thank them for stepping up and intervening. We had the chance to express how we hoped this segment would tell a story the world needed. The world desperately needed more heroes like them who support LGBTQ+ youth when they are being bullied. They all understood and were happy to participate in something that would be so impactful.

Once the segment aired, it blew up immediately. The show posted the segment on their YouTube page, and it skyrocketed to millions of views. This was just mere months after the Supreme Court ruling in the Obergefell v. Hodges case in June 2015. This ruling gave same-sex couples the fundamental right to marry at the federal level. Tensions were still high for the population on both sides of the argument for marriage equality. Our segment was one of the very few LGBTQ+ segments they had ever aired on *WWYD?*, and it proved to be popular with LGBTQ+ youth and allies. All of the gay publications and blogs wrote about it. Those articles and clips of the show were shared millions of times across all social platforms.

Within a few weeks, I gained thousands of Instagram followers. Mostly young people who saw the segment and were thankful to see people like them talking through issues they were trying to LIVE through. I received so many messages from these people thanking me for being a good representation of an LGBTQ+ person, thanking me for showing them that it's okay for them to be gay. And some simply thanked me for just being present and talking to them. They had no one else to talk to.

I was now suddenly burdened by this huge responsibility of being a role model for all of these young people, and I was terrified. Going into this project, I never could have imagined it would be this big. I never asked for or expected to receive this mantle. But I knew that I had to at least try. I thought of how much I would've loved to see a gay guy on the Internet when I was younger. Social media didn't exist. I wasn't able to have a connection to anyone that had a life like the one I wished for myself. I didn't want these young people to go through the same thing. Representation matters. It matters so much.

To this day, I still try to talk to every single person that messages me on Instagram. And for those that ask questions or need help, I do my best to provide my personal answer while also pointing them to resources that are probably a much better source of reliable information. Sometimes, I just tell them my personal experience. To let them know I've been there, too. They are definitely not alone. Things will get better, and they will one day be more in charge of their lives and surroundings.

There are some who didn't know who to talk to about feeling suicidal. They didn't know what to do, where to get help, or even if help was available. There is a lot to be extra careful of in the world of social media, but for the most part, I'm very thankful for it. Without this ability to find your community, no matter where you are in the world, there would be so much more pain, loneliness, and darkness.

Many of these people have become lifelong Internet friends. I get to keep up with them on Instagram. It's always so nice to see them come into their own. Blossom into the being that they were meant to be, one that they now love. They fully accept themselves, have their own boyfriends or girlfriends, and have found their way through those bleak times.

I never thought that I would ever be in this type of a position, but I guess when life asks you to do more, you put on your hustle boots and make it happen. It's my duty to help the next generations like those before helped me. Also, the whole thing has definitely made me a better person. I now work to be the person that the next generation needs. The person that I so desperately needed.

It's incredibly difficult sometimes, but I just feel like I HAVE to do this. I have to work at it every single day. It's too important not to. The hustle is real! But the LGBTQ+ community has such a rich legacy of the older helping the younger and seeing them through the tough and challenging times. I'm grateful I get to participate in that legacy in some way. Hopefully one day, someone I helped will go on to help the next generation, and that legacy will continue on for generations to come.

KEEP GROWING

AFTER ONE OF my best Cluemaster friends quit the job for a better offer, I was stuck wondering how I was going to get through this job every night until one in the morning, making enough money to live, and getting enough sleep to make it to that call to sign up for the next audition at seven in the morning. While I no longer had to wait around at the audition for a chance to be seen, there was still the crack-of-dawn sign-up madness. An actor's life is full of these sacrifices, which makes it seem *cool*, I guess, but sometimes it just plain sucks! For the better part of a year, I definitely felt like I had joined Team Rocket, failing every day to succeed, or at the very least, taking one step forward in my mission.

My abandoner left for a job with an immersive theatre company that had recently made a huge name for itself. Third Rail Projects had been around for a while, gaining momentum as a dance company started in the early 2000s by three ambitious creators: Jennine Willett, Zach Morris, and Tom Pearson. Ever curious about how performance can shape a person and how performance can better reach audiences in a meaningful way, they broke from the existing barrier of concert-type dance performances and started creating site-specific theatre. Not necessarily a new thing in the world of performance, but rather a theatrical form that had been somewhat lost along the way, as movies and television dominated the last century of entertainment.

Third Rail Projects now rejected all categorical conventions in favor of pure performance in any medium that served the work. They exist in this nebulous, genre-fluid place of art making. Sometimes they were very dance heavy, other times more proscenium theatre, and sometimes just multi-sensory experiences. Flavors that were traditionally kept distant were now married and fed to the audience by hand.

These three would go to an assortment of different sites and create a work specifically for the mood, lighting, and architecture of that unique, particular space. These artists would enter into these industrial, public landscapes and ignite the entire space into life. Third Rail Projects has a very exquisite way of making these forgotten spaces sing with their own voice, with their own history. A testament to finding the extraordinary in the often overlooked or disregarded in the hustle and bustle of everyday life. Bringing these live performances into non-traditional places also meant the audiences were largely made up of people who don't normally see performances or dance. It was another clever way to spread art into the world.

In 2012, the company shot to notoriety with their hit show, *Then She Fell*. *Then She Fell* was a fully immersive experience set against the backdrop of Lewis Carroll's writings and his real-life relationship with the young Alice Liddell, the inspiration for *Alice in Wonderland*. Only fifteen audience members per performance could attend, and they spent two hours exploring a three-story, old hospital ward that had been completely built into the set of this show. In the experience, the audience members would explore the rooms of this hospital, often by themselves or with one or two fellow audience members in tow, all while the performance happened around them, and more importantly, with them. They'd discover hidden scenes, encounter performers one-on-one, and unearth clues that illuminated a haunting story. Also throughout the performance, audience members were handed different cocktails that were custom designed just for the show. A little imbibing to free the senses, if you will.

After hearing about this unbelievable concept, I begged my friend to help me get a ticket! As you can imagine, with only fifteen audience members per performance, the show's ticket price was quite high, and they sold out weeks in advance, easily. Through some serious hustling, I was able to score a single ticket to a performance at ten thirty on a Tuesday evening. Prime theatre-going time for poor folks, for sure! Armed with this single golden ticket, I set off by myself to the mythical land of Brooklyn for this performance, not quite sure what to expect and definitely not knowing how much this single, crisp fall night would change my life forever.

As soon as I entered the hospital ward, I was greeted by "hospital staff" who checked me in, then a kind orderly handed me my first dose of medicine. I obediently sipped, and off I slipped into the most lucid dream, filled with the most gorgeous images. Fragments of a story that we, the audience, almost remembered together in real-time. I remembered, or maybe dreamt, a seductive dance in a stairwell, a haunting duet in a mirror that wasn't really there, the most dangerously chaotic tea party, a steel cold doctor's visit, and the horror of a woman's mental breakdown, feet away from me. I never woke up from that liminal space that night, even as I ventured back home and eventually slipped off into a much more corporeal sleep. It was, simply put, unreal, in every best sense of the word.

I found myself dreaming, pondering, and meditating on *Then She Fell* for weeks after that night. I sung its praises to anyone who would let me rant about it. Discussions that stuck to themes, magic, and experiences, leaving out the details so as not to spoil it, for they MUST see it for themselves. Almost like those who live through an extraterrestrial event, I was certain people thought I was crazy, but I would find a community of those who had also experienced the abduction into *Then She Fell*'s world. We understood each other; those who hadn't seen it could never understand.

Then She Fell proved to be a massive turning point for Third Rail Projects. They had elevated themselves to a pinnacle in this unknown territory of immersive theatre. Right around this same time, another virally-famous immersive theatre production opened: *Sleep No More*. *Sleep No More* mixed a film noir world with Shakespeare's *Macbeth* and set dozens of audience members free to mingle with performers in a vast multi-story warehouse in the heart of Manhattan. Third Rail Projects was detonating along with this huge immersive theatre boom in New York City. And as people were being drawn further into the world of technology that tends to keep us separated, staring at screens, these new experiences demanded the connection that we as humans crave on a primal level. Whether modern audiences knew it or not, it was an ancient salve to the modern-day world.

After a few talks with my guy on the inside, expressing my passion to work with this company, I landed the first job that would start the most incredible journey. *Then She Fell* received a rave review in *The New York Times* by Ben Brantley, and with the long extensions that continued to sell out, Third Rail Projects opened up to the world. They were commissioned to make new site-specific works around the globe, collecting more of a following, gathering more fans. Everywhere they went, people would clamor about how amazing the experience was, how enthralling they made everything seem, and how touching and poetic the scenes unfolded. *The Grand Paradise*, their next big New York City project, would be an accumulation of a few previous works, built on a massive scale. Set in the 1970s at a beach resort, the story lines of a whole family would get entangled in dreams, hopes, wishes, and even death. This time, the show would accommodate an audience of sixty per performance, so it would need a few extra hands for its greater scale.

I started working for them as the "front door guy" for *The Grand Paradise* when it opened in January of 2016. Every single night, I would happily check in all guests for both performances, make sure that they checked their coats and bags, and usher them into the performance as seamlessly as possible. It was seemingly very low grunt work, but I started to appreciate it as one of the most vital necessities on a production such as this. Some nights I'd be more of a host, and other nights I would end up being more of a bouncer, having to kick out a few unruly patrons with all five feet, five inches and one hundred ten pounds of my being.

I was more than happy to do it all because I fell in love with this company. I just so needed to be around them to continue feeding my soul and witnessing this artistry. If I wanted to grow into an artist of this caliber, I needed to learn as much as possible. And I couldn't do that if I didn't surround myself with them. Plus, it beat the soul-sucking job of waiting tables any night of the week, and it still allowed me to keep my days free while auditioning and working gigs.

Over time, I grew closer to the company and became one of them. The friend that folded me into this world left, and I took on the mantle of his position overseeing the box office of *Then She Fell*. Making sure the show maintained itself financially. Organizing group events, and managing audience relations. Then that position would grow with the company, moving me into an even larger role, with the most responsibilities I've ever had at a single job.

In addition to these duties, I moved into a more communications-based role. I helped in the marketing department for the entire company, ran the social media initiatives, coordinated the box office systems with our co-presenters of projects, and even became the first person of contact for potential collaborations. The artistic directors trusted me to properly vet all incoming inquiries and gather the information necessary to see if a partnership may be possible. Best of all, the entire company understood the necessary juggling of an artists› lifestyle. I was still able to audition, take acting work, and be in shows, as long as I was able to get all of my work done, which was never a problem. It was the perfect day job for a performer.

Somehow along the way, I was given a seat at the table with some of the greatest minds in the entire immersive theatre industry. My insights on audience experience, from the point of ticket purchase to entering the performance, were relied upon when building new works. Sometimes even my thoughts on the performance itself were considered, some taken, some not, but it was a truly collaborative process. How did I even get here? It's what I worked toward, but it happened so subtly over a thousand little actions that I must have missed the moment of change. Sometimes, even years after my first cold night at the door, I would be in a meeting and just stop and stare at the three artistic directors talking to me, asking my opinion on company matters, or seeking my help to solve a problem, and I would get that lucid dream feeling again.

Each of the three artistic directors holds a specific pillar in the company, providing the structure for the rest of the machine to operate. Tom Pearson, the mind, has an ever growing curiosity about the big questions of the universe and humanity. He's stoic in his deep, trancelike meditations on death, dreams, rituals, and connection. Devoted to a life of learning, his brain operates on such a high level that one might consider him Professor X in this school of artists, if you will. His ability to connect every single story, event, or religion to the greater tapestry of the (capital) Human Experience is a spectacle.

Zach Morris, the body, is a man of action through and through. Fueled by an insatiable desire to create, he must never stop moving or else he very well might die. Incessantly working on multiple projects at once, he employs all of his most trusted artists as if they were his own limbs to pump as much art out into the world as he can. Desperate to use what little time he has on Earth, to make it, maybe, just a little bit better.

And perhaps the most enigmatic of the three, Jennine Willett is clearly the soul. Binding everyone together into the family that is Third Rail Projects, she is the matriarch herself. With a deafening gentleness, her presence alone makes one feel completely safe, or better yet, hopeful. With a passion for education and a life's mission of cultivating future generations of artists, she does all she can for the future. She's perhaps the most noble of all of us. And yet, her secret weapon lies in the pure strength she doesn't necessarily keep on display. Her business acumen, expert negotiation skills, and the fierce guardianship she bestows upon the company are magnificent. I'm forever fascinated by the dualities she contains. I can't help but ponder on how growing up as a woman throughout the '70s and '80s might have influenced the flawless code-switching skills she possesses today. I wish more people got to see the absolute boss bitch she is.

Rarely do you ever get a chance to be treated as an equal by a boss. But since everyone on staff was so used to the collaborative environment that it takes to build a show, the artistic directors took the same approach in their business tactics. Of course, my superiors still assigned me duties. But even still, I always felt like an equal. Equally important, equally valued, and my thoughts equally weighed. It was a breath of fresh air that I wish for more organizations.

While I settled into my position with them on the theatre administration side, it would be a few years before I joined their ranks as a performer. Again, their particular niche in performance was different than mine, so I wasn't sure if I would even fit in. Then came the summer of 2019, when Third Rail Projects was collaborating with another production company, Food Of Love, to co-produce an immersive revival of *A Midsummer Night's Dream*. This was the first time since I had been with the company that they were doing a performance that was more actor-based, as opposed to their more dance-based usual. They were definitely going to need top-tier Shakespearean actors for this production. I absolutely *knew* I had the acting training for this, and I was very confident in my Shakespeare skills. Plus, I absolutely adore *A Midsummer Night's Dream*, having been in multiple productions during my school years. If ever I was going to get the chance to show my skills to this company, it was going to be in this production. I was willing to do anything to book this!

When they held auditions, I wasn't able to get an appointment for the life of me (a fact that I still remain salty about to this day)! If you don't get a direct audition appointment, an actor is forced to rely on an open call for a chance to be seen. Instead of just showing up at your appointment, auditioning, and being on your way, an open call is an all-day, energy-draining endeavor. You get up at the crack of dawn to put your name on a list to claim a two-minute-maximum audition slot. Nothing is guaranteed, and you often have to wait around for hours with the energy vampires that are desperate actors.

Getting an audition appointment is elusive in some cases,

due to many factors. Fine. But here I was, an Equity actor who had proven myself as a reliable individual in my work capacity, and who already had a solid resume of performance work under my belt, still denied. My agent tried and failed. I wasn't even able to secure a pity "courtesy appointment" from my dear friend and mentor, the man who was helming this production as director, Zach Morris. Look, maybe in this instance my feelings make me an entitled little jerk, but as I'll say forever, I'm not perfect, and not getting an initial appointment felt like a slap in the face. One that stung like hell.

At that point, my survival instincts kicked in, forcing me to rely on the learned techniques from my past. I was going to need to try harder and be smarter than any of the rest of my competition. I had slipped a little and expected to be handed something. That's someone else's life, not mine. I needed to work for what I wanted!

Instead of wallowing in that hurt for long, I bundled it up and used it to fuel my next move. Though it was admittedly not the healthiest take on the situation, I was determined to prove myself at the open call. I intended to show up and be so damn good that they would realize their mistake. I wanted to let that chip on my shoulder grow into a boulder. More so, I wanted them to be embarrassed that they passed me over the first time. In my perfectly petty picture of the possible outcomes, I would even turn down the offer of a role after wasting their time by auditioning.

After letting the more nefarious of those thoughts pass, I held on to the motivation my little chip gave me, and I woke up entirely too early on a Monday morning to make my way to the open call audition, in hopes that I would be seen. Finally, my name was called, and I was ushered into the audition room at nine thirty-five that morning. After a few rounds of callbacks, and a weekend of deliberations, my agent called that next Monday to let me know that I booked it! My first Off-Broadway show!

Not only did I get to work with artists that I absolutely adored, including the newly-forgiven director Zach Morris, but the cast received top-notch dance and movement training from the incomparable Julia Kelly and Edward Rice, two of my top favorite performers of all time. These two are just absolutely amazing at their game, and more importantly, at teaching. Their level of understanding a body — its structure, its muscles, ligaments, and needs — is astounding. Things that only the top athletes would know. And I swear to GOD, they whipped the entire cast into shape as if we were training for the Olympics!

This production of *A Midsummer Night's Dream* was performed with only eight performers, each of us playing at least three roles each. Set in a fanciful 1920s French influenced café that we dubbed Café Fae, we created environmental staging all around the audience. The audience sat at tables throughout the space, while us performers weaved in and out between them for scenes, dances, and even fights. Right off Union Square, this space was built out beautifully, and even featured a full kitchen backstage, because, oh yeah, we were also serving a multi-course meal with wine during the performance. And when I say we, I mean WE, the performers.

This new *Midsummer: A Banquet* also featured a world-building, thirty-minute pre-show process to seat patrons, serve them their first course, and get them ready for the entire experience. We served, sang, welcomed, danced, and played instruments, all to wow an audience and blur the line between character and real human performer, strengthening the connection we could all have together in this magical place. How Actors' Equity let us do all that, I'll never know, but I'm so glad they did.

After the pre-show, the scripted performance began. We switched gears for a full, two-hour Shakespearean show where we were flipping over tables, lifting each other, dodging in tables and chairs of audience members, still serving more food, completing a hundred costume changes, and engaging as many of our patrons' senses as we could. A favorite moment of the show was filling the house with applewood smoke.

One course was these delicious vegetable skewers, served in mason jars that were filled with applewood smoke right before they were sealed shut. So, as audience members opened the jars, the magical smoke would rise up from the jar before their eyes, and the entire house filled with a smoky cloud that smelled like the forest campfire where our scene was set. Zach Morris' genius is in his attention to the details that really make a performance magical. He worked with food designer Emilie Baltz to really make the production work as a whole and give the audience these little surprises throughout. This thoughtfulness translated into a Drama Desk Award nomination!

This project was my Off-Broadway debut, and I couldn't have been prouder. For those who don't know, in the realm of New York City acting contracts, there is Broadway, and then right under that, there's Off-Broadway. It's probably the most prestigious contract I have gotten to work on in my career thus far, and it really made me believe in myself again as a competitive actor.

I really had the chance to sink my teeth into complex roles that I don't normally get to play. Normally, due to my small size, ethnicity, or whatever other dumb characteristic directors don't like, I've never had the chance to play a leading man type role. I'm either asked to be the nerdy side character, or the street druggie (because, you know, LATINO!). Because of all of these reasons, I never saw myself ever playing Demetrius, one of the four core lovers in this play. I had grown too comfortable playing those funny, whacky, secondary characters, and I refused to go in for any more "street, urban guys." I'd always felt like I could play this role, but to actually be given the chance was a blessing, if not a little scary.

And because it was a three-hour show of non-stop moving, dancing, fighting, lifting, and flipping, my body went THROUGH it. I never thought I'd become *that* person, but here I was in my twenties, wishing I had had my teenage body back. This show was an ultimate physical test in how to do eight shows a week. I felt myself grow so much stronger mentally, physically, and emotionally. I wouldn't trade anything like that for the world.

To my *Midsummer* family: I love you, and I'll always love you. Since it was so incredibly unique, this show definitely bonded us all forever. All of the good, and all of the struggles we went through to make this insane idea of a show come to life. I cannot wait to see what Third Rail Projects does next. Hopefully, I'll be around for many more adventures and grand works of art.

They say, "You are who you hang out with," and I believe that to be true. I have always had a strong desire to be surrounded by those at the top of their craft. After all, how are you supposed to get better at something without those around to teach you? When a moment comes along to be in the midst of giants, I hope you take the chance to do so. I hope you dive in wholeheartedly, because sometimes that moment spins into years of wonderful adventures, learning, and growth.

However, these steps often don't look like dives. They can sometimes be a lateral step or even a step back that gets us in the door. I never thought that working check-in at a show would grow to be such a huge part of my life, but it did. And while I worked to prove myself to Third Rail Projects, I do owe so much of my growth as a theatre administrator, as an artist, and simply just as a human being to this amazing collective of people that are now my family. So, if you ever find yourself near one of Third Rail Projects' productions, please check it out! And tell them I sent you!

KEEP SWEET

WITH A SMALL but growing audience on the Internet from being on national television, I quickly grew passionate about creating content. I love entertaining, I love making people smile, and I had proof in my inbox that I could help so many people the more I shared my story. In theatre, we share stories to accomplish all of these same goals. While showbiz is fickle and I couldn't always be in a show, I had found an outlet that was so similar. One that I had a lot more control over. And one that wasn't financially dependent on being all that popular. I could post what I wanted. I had complete creative control.

A huge reason why I create content and share my life on social media is so that the world, and those who really need it, can see a gay Latino in their feeds every once in a while. Making sure I put myself, my life, and my work out there as much as possible so that it's SEEN. So that I'M SEEN. So that another gay Latino boy growing up knows that he too can be SEEN! Plus, I love finding ways I can help make the world a better place, while sharing, caring, and spreading more love on the Internet. We all know it needs it.

One of these content creation adventures was *Sweet Husbands TV*: a YouTube series where Matt and I would post reviews about desserts from bakeries and shops we would find all around New York City. We would travel to the shop, take secret footage of our experience, buy a few treats, and head back home. Once home, we would dig into our confectionary loot and review the entire experience. Everything from customer service, flavor, pastrymanship, and price point was reviewed, in an effort to find the best establishments that New York City had to offer. This show wasn't very successful in the number of views, but we would forever be monikered as "The Sweet Husbands," a title I can definitely get behind. And it gave birth to our catchphrase that we will always be able to carry with us: "Keep Sweet!"

Now, one thing everyone should know about me is that I absolutely love baked goods! I love pastries, donuts, cookies, cakes, and anything that has sugar and has been inside an oven. There is nothing better than planning to get a sweet treat after a big audition, meeting, or presentation. Because you can always go! If the audition went well and you got a callback, then you MUST celebrate by getting that delicious cupcake. If the meeting went wrong and you may be fired soon, well, nothing will make you feel better like biting into a warm, gooey chocolate chip cookie the size of your face!

One day, Matt and I found this cute little bakery, simply named CHOCnyc, in our Inwood neighborhood. It was a brand new patisserie, boasting a sleek new sign, just on the corner right next to the A train's entrance. This place was unlike anything in the area. The head chef was a French pastry chef, trained at the highest level the French pastry world offers. And he was serving all the traditional confections one might find in ol' gay Paris. The pastry case was filled with various croissants, macarons, tarts, and even truffles, all handcrafted on-site by this chef and his very select team of professionals. Each item looked better than the last, and it was hard to choose which to select. Did I go for the three-layer carrot cake or the gold leaf-adorned eclair?

My first victim would be the chocolate croissant. The chocolate croissant is always my litmus test when testing out a new bakery. And this one was the best one I've ever encountered in the hundreds that have met their fate in my belly. The outside was perfectly browned, and there were seemingly a million layers in this expertly laminated dough. Upon first bite, I felt the absolute perfect crispness give way to an impossibly soft, warm, and buttery inside. The key to a good croissant is a lot of butter, and they did not skimp at all. The texture was perfect — light and airy, not dense and bready. And last but not least, the chocolate elevated the experience to the divine realm. Three rods of solid, rich chocolate. Not overly sweet, but in perfect harmony with the buttery pastry. After that first bite, I was hooked! This pain au chocolat would become my new pan du jour!

After this transcendent experience, we felt it was our duty to inform everyone about this hidden uptown gem. We hated that it was probably being overshadowed by so many shops that had made a name for themselves but were selling inferior products at much higher prices. So, being the creative and entertaining people that we are, we decided to start a little

YouTube series. We didn't know what we were doing, and we didn't have any fancy equipment. Using just our iPhones, editing in iMovie, and uploading ourselves, *Sweet Husbands TV* was born. Plus, Matt and I love working together and didn't have much going on at the time. It gave us a way to spend time together, and of course, a reason to eat more scrumptious treats!

Originally, *Sweet Husbands TV* was only meant to be for our family and friends, all of whom knew of our deep addiction to sugar, and most of whom had received a personalized dessert tour from us while they were visiting from out of town. We wanted to share some of our life in New York City with them and create a catalog of places to take them whenever they came back to the city. We never had any expectation of it becoming widely viewed. I think that's what took all of the pressure off and kept the experience fun and fulfilling for us.

While it didn't become a huge viral sensation, *Sweet Husbands TV* did receive more attention than we originally thought. A few hundred subscribers and thousands of views paled in comparison to a new level of social identity we'd find. While we definitely knew not all of our friends and acquaintances watched our episodes, every single person still knew that this series was happening. Any time we would meet up with a friend, they gushed about their favorite video. Or how they, too, loved Schmackary's cookies over Levain's.

I think it was a testament to Matt's marketing prowess, specifically in the area of branding. While they might not have watched a video, people knew who the Sweet Husbands were, and what they were all about. There were even times when I would walk into an audition, and the casting director would ask if I had eaten any really good cookies or donuts lately. It was eye opening to see that it could have such an impact. There was a level of awareness that people had about us that wasn't there before.

What was most interesting to me about this experiment was how much value it gave us, even without meeting the standard parameters of success. Well, at least those parameters that we have been conditioned to think mark a project's success. First, we never made a single cent on any of our videos. Though sometimes we would receive free treats and invitations to big events, we never actually received any financial gain.

Secondly, *Sweet Husbands TV* wouldn't even be considered very successful according to YouTube's own standards. While we did receive a decent amount of views for a budding channel, they weren't too noteworthy. They weren't astronomical, or unusually high, and worse yet, they didn't convert well into subscribers. For as long as we focused on pushing out this content, we never got over a few hundred subscribers. Still hundreds away from the bare minimum needed to even have a chance of being monetized on YouTube. But there were still plenty gains to be had!

Matt honed his marketing skills. He learned and adapted to every Internet platform out there, with his pieces of content getting more and more engagement. Skills that would later on make him a star at VaynerMedia. I got to hone my hosting skills by working on-camera over and over again, during a time that was very slow for me career-wise. These videos of me on camera would even go on to help me get auditions and work in the commercial world. And it kept me on the minds of casting directors that followed me on social media. It was a huge gain in social capital that I couldn't have predicted.

Sadly, *Sweet Husbands TV* has been cancelled for now. But it drew me further into this fascinating world of creating, entertaining, and engaging with people on the Internet. These were all things that I knew I loved doing in a live performance setting, but I didn't know that I could just as easily be fulfilled through a digital platform. This new world has become an important facet of who I am as an artist, running equally parallel to my career in the "real world."

Even financially, content creation gigs are usually far more beneficial for me than a traditional commercial job as an actor, which I find fascinating. Usually for these lower end commercial jobs, I'll have to go in for an audition. The auditions at times can be stressful, and each one costs me about an hour or two of my time when you factor in getting ready, taking the subway, and waiting in the lobby. I'll probably book one of these jobs for every fifteen to twenty auditions I go on.

Then I have to go work a full day on set to film the job. The average pay I have received for one of these jobs is probably around one thousand dollars. Once paid, ten percent goes immediately to my agent, leaving me with nine hundred dollars before taxes. For my content creation gigs or brand partnerships on Instagram, I have been paid comparable rates, maybe a bit less, but for a tiny fraction of the amount of time and work it takes on my part.

Plus, I have much more say in who I get to work with.

I don't have to worry about getting dropped by my agent because I don't want to film a commercial for a scummy credit card company that preys on people. I can take work that pays a little less for a company whose mission I believe in. And I'm able to take less money because I don't have to invest very many hours or effort on my end. They are benefitting from my platform and the skills I've acquired in making content for them.

But my love for making content will never go away. I still think it is as important as ever to make sure I keep putting forth myself as a LGBTQ+ individual in a loving, gay marriage as much as possible. This identity has been vilified for far too long for me to not do my part to change how the world perceives people like me. I know the hatred comes from fear, and fear comes from unknowing. The haters usually just need to be exposed to us to see that we aren't so bad after all. So I will go on exposing myself as much as possible... wait...

It's unavoidable to realize that the majority of the #instagay influencers are a certain *type*. Caucasian, huge pecs, six-pack abs, and arms that are as big as my entire torso. It works for them, and if I had that package, I would definitely use it to my advantage. But if those of us who look different don't try to get to the same level, it will never happen. And so we have to keep trying, even if we are left with just ten percent of the attention, followers, and brand deals, that's still a step toward progress. Progress I'm starting to see happen, and that gets me so excited!

Along with trying to inject some desperately needed diversity into the #instagay influencer scene, I am also committed to doling out hefty doses of positivity. There are so many ways social media can make us feel worse about our lives. Comparing ourselves to others, playing with our mental health issues or body dysmorphia, but I have witnessed the good that this type of connection can bring. And I'm determined to try and keep my content as close to a panacea as possible. Even if it's not "deep" or "thought provoking," I think lighthearted positivity can be just as important.

We all need a little sweet treat to get us through our days. That episode of a silly show that makes us smile. That romcom that may not get any Oscar nominations but will be watched a million more times because of how it makes us feel. That musical that ends in a huge dance party. It's clear that these fluff pieces are an integral part to our lives as human beings. It's clear how much more we consume the saccharine art over the prestigious. Like kids with cotton candy, we smile big, as it heals our souls.

KEEP HOPE

ONCE I MOVED to New York City, I knew that the only neighborhood that I wanted to live in, one of the few that I could actually afford to live in, was Washington Heights. As any MT Gay (MT stands for musical theatre, and is, of course, a label given to those fledgling actors), knows, Washington Heights was lit! The birthplace, and hometown if you will, of THE Lin-Manuel Miranda. I just had to live there. Plus, as a Latino moving away from Texas, it proved to be a safe haven for me in my beginning years in New York City. Seeing all the people that looked like me and spoke Spanish really made me feel like I was somewhat home in this scary new place. A place that would become less scary and become my actual home.

Now, I did end up living in Washington Heights for many years, and I absolutely loved it. It was a perfect distance away from the hustle and bustle of the midtown epicenter but was still always bustling with life. A spirit that my country-boy soul had been craving all along in a neighborhood.

Maybe one day I'll find myself back there, but for now, I'll always remember it fondly, like an old friend, who was great but we just drifted apart. And by drifted apart, I mean the opportunity of a lifetime was dropped in our laps and we just had to take it.

You see, New York City is a wannabe progressive mecca, and yet housing costs are out of this world and completely unaffordable for the working class that make this city run. Without these people, it would be hard for lower-paying, menial labor jobs to be filled. A problem that the rich oligarchs actually sort of care about. One small answer to that problem is the New York City affordable housing lotteries. The city gives these huge tax breaks to new apartment building developments, but in exchange, the buildings have to offer a certain number of apartment units at a lower rate for the "poor people." Otherwise known as all of those who are working full-time jobs or multiple part-time jobs and still aren't able to afford rent. #capitalism. And I, lifelong "poor kid," always dreamed of the day when I'd be able to crash in a luxury apartment. I just didn't think that it would be thanks in part to some government program I would, as a starving artist, qualify for.

As soon as we moved to the city, Matt and I began applying for every single housing lottery we qualified for. For those wondering, there is a central website as part of the nyc.gov website. Once there, you fill out a simple application regarding your household size, income, and current living situation. Then, as new lotteries become available, you simply submit that one application to all of the building lotteries that you could potentially qualify for before the submission deadline.

Be sure to keep your application as up-to-date as possible, and be sure to check the website regularly. Most lotteries have a submission window of about a month or two.

Then, once the submission deadline has passed, the system generates a random number to every single application sent in. This is called a log number. Of course, the number of applicants varies from lottery to lottery, but generally, you can expect to be given a number from one to fifty thousand. For this particular story, we were given a log number of one thousand, thirty-three. One of my new favorite numbers.

Reading the New York City housing lottery forums (yes, there are forums out there), we knew that any number in the low thousands is a good number. Once everyone has a log number, caseworkers begin the monumental task of going through every single application starting from number one. Now, about ninety percent of applications are immediately thrown out, as they do not actually qualify for the lottery due to a variety of reasons; remember to keep those applications up-to-date! They look at the income information you put on your application to make cuts during this first round. So, if it's not up-to-date, you can be erroneously cut and lost in the cycle of appeals because your income situation recently changed.

Once they have enough folks they believe can qualify, they call them in, in order, for what they call "interviews." Once you make it to the interview step, your odds are very good, so long as you are telling the truth and do all of the grunt work to provide them all of the proof they need. And holy cow is it so much proof. Which is fair. They are offering you a dream of an apartment at an incredibly low rate, oftentimes similar to what you were paying for your shitty apartment that most likely should be condemned.

After living in New York City and applying for years, one March, we received notice that we'd be moving to the interview process for a beautiful, brand-new, luxury apartment in midtown Manhattan. I *still* haven't stopped screaming. My friends just wear noise-canceling headphones and know not to take me out in public. Even just knowing that there could be a CHANCE of actually living in a place like that was entirely overwhelming.

While they call it an "interview," it's more of an informal meeting to turn in all of your paperwork. ALL of your paperwork. They request almost every single piece of paper that has ever had your name on it. All forms of identification, utility bills, birth certificates, social security cards, leases, months of bank statements, savings accounts, tax returns, letters of employment, that one page in Lesley's notebook where I wrote "Joshua wuz here" in sixth grade.

Luckily, I married the most type-A gay man in the world, and not only did he tirelessly put all of the documents together, but he completely organized the material into a single binder. Complete with dividers, tabs, labels, everything to make it easy for the auditors to get whatever information they desired the fastest. At the interview, this binder made an excellent first impression. The managers knew we were responsible, had our shit together, and would be able to provide everything they needed for the process.

For this particular building, there were nineteen apartments available, and they had called in fifty people for the first round of these interviews. Now they do go in numerical order, so we had to cross our fingers and hope that, as the process continued over the next few months, thirty-one people would be disqualified for whatever reason and that there would still be an apartment for us. Because we, of course, were number fifty.

What followed that interview were six agonizing months of waiting. Not hearing anything for weeks, then a phone call! You have to answer immediately or they'll move on, and there isn't a way to call them back. Usually, the phone call would have a small update, "You are still in the running," and then an action, "We need this new paper signed and back to us immediately." Six months of hoping, wishing, praying, and the occasional burst of dropping everything to run a form to an employer. Run to a notary to get another form notarized. A call to our management company for lease copies, whatever. But a call at least meant that we still had a chance.

The worst part of this experience was a feeling as if we were frozen in time. An actor's life is very unpredictable. Oftentimes, you audition for gigs that work within the month and pay out at the end of the month or the next month. But accepting another job from another employer and adding wages to my income could throw a huge monkey wrench into the whole process. It was already complicated enough, but if I added anything new, it may have caused our application to stall, slow, or get disqualified. So, I couldn't do anything. I stopped auditioning and just waited. Turned down auditions for things I would die to be a part of. It felt like an eternity, and I started to lose a little bit of my identity and who I was as an artist, but I knew that the sacrifice would be worth it. It had to be worth it.

On the opposite end of the spectrum, we also couldn't really go out and spend any money. We had to be ready at the drop of a hat to fork over a first month's rent, a deposit, moving expenses, and a possible month's rent at our current place if we couldn't find a subletter or get out of our lease. Without being able to change our income or expenses, we kind of couldn't really do anything. And when you aren't as busy, you have more time to just sit and think. Not think, daydream. Wonder, worry, hope, pray. It was not a great place to be in for so long.

Then one day, we got the best call ever. It was our turn for an apartment. It was happening, and—what luck—it was the LAST apartment available! We had just barely made the cut-off, but it was finally our turn. I couldn't believe it! All my wildest dreams were coming true. My entire life taught me that nothing is certain until you are standing inside that apartment, holding the key. So, we proceeded hastily, but I still tried to not get my hopes up. It was already so unbelievable, maybe I wasn't quite believing it myself. All we had to do was schedule a tour of the apartment, schedule a lease signing with the office, and the apartment would be ours.

The next day, we got gut-punched full force. Another call. Another application that had previously been denied submitted an appeal for their denial. By law, that means that any application with a higher log number has been halted until the appeal process is over. Back to the waiting period we went. The rollercoaster was coming to an end one way or the other, and the emotional ups and downs were getting to me, hard. I found myself just praying for it to be over. Whether or not we got the apartment anymore, I almost didn't care. I just needed the anxiety-ridden depressive state to be over. I had never experienced, and still haven't experienced, such an emotional toll like I did from this process.

The universe was proctoring its cruel test out on me. I knew it, and I just forfeited the right to get to decide. I gave up the outcome, let go of the selfish want I had for the apartment, told God that whatever he wanted would happen. I would accept it and move on accordingly. Once that release happened, I found myself again. The process wasn't over, but I remembered who I was. I had been living a great life in our current living situation. I had so much to be grateful and thankful for. Who was I to ask for more? To dote endlessly on the possibility of something I did nothing to deserve? I kept my hope that it could happen, but I had truly found what hope means. My hoping transformed from wishing, lusting, and desiring this wonderful thing, into being grateful for the opportunity, looking for ways to be generous with the gift if I received it. I looked at how I could serve people with the apartment, should I be given the responsibility of it.

About two weeks later, I was walking underground transferring between subway lines on my way to Brooklyn for work. I had my wired headphones in, listening to some podcast, probably the latest serial killer story from *My Favorite Murder*, when I got a phone call from my husband. As I took the call, I marveled at how he caught me at the exact right time. For those that don't know, cell phone service doesn't work very well on the subway, oftentimes making phone calls absolutely impossible while traveling deep underground. But for this specific instance, I was a little more above ground, having just stepped off of a train and walking to another. Just in reach of the cell signal to take the call.

Matt quickly let me know that we were not alone on the call. Our housing caseworker was also on the line. I froze. Everything around me slowed down. The entire bustle of New York City commuters on the way to work, school, or to Whole Foods became entirely drowned out by this woman's every word. She was less than three words in when I caught the slightest spark of joy in her voice. The instant my ears picked up on that bright tone, my eyes unleashed a flood of tears matched only by Viola Davis (in every single project she's ever been in).

The opposing applicant's appeal didn't get approved, and we were back in the running. This time, though, it was unlikely there would be any other appeals that could head our way before we were able to sign the lease. The gigantic sense of relief was welcomed, but it wasn't over, not yet. The earliest they could get us in to view the apartment was in a few hours. Matt couldn't go, but I could be given full authority to sign off. I arrived at work, just long enough to tell them the news, settle myself down, and turn right back around to meet the housing manager for the apartment viewing. I met the lovely gentleman who would be showing me around the apartment outside the building, and I practically made him race me upstairs to give me a tour.

The apartment was absolutely gorgeous. Nestled on the thirty-third floor of a beautiful building overlooking midtown Manhattan through floor-to-ceiling glass and steel windows. Brand-new appliances, with the refrigerator, freezer, and the dishwasher hidden within the cabinets. The washer and dryer had their own little closet. THE WASHER AND DRYER! Due to the age of many of New York's apartment buildings, washers and dryers are extremely rare. Up until now, Matt and I had yet to have either in one of our New York apartments. And of course, the holy grail of apartment amenities: central heat and air conditioning.

For those unacquainted, central air conditioning in New York is the pipe dream for people's apartments. The majority of apartments come with a standard window and radiator controlled by the building. This means that during the warmer months, you are desperately trying to not sweat to death by opening windows, installing a three-ton window air conditioner without killing anyone on the street, and avoiding using the oven at all costs. But during the winter months, you are at the mercy of your landlord to turn on the radiators. Forever manipulating the temperature between sauna and freezer by less than a quarter-turn of a twist on the radiator valve, and being lulled to sleep by the clinkity-clangity binks and bangs of the pipes. Central air is a fable you heard of once upon a time, in your ancient past or in another life.

After exactly one minute of confirming that all of the mythical features were present in the apartment and that it looked exactly like the pictures that Matt and I had fawned over for MONTHS, I tried bullying the gentleman of a leasing agent into letting us sign the lease that evening once Matt got off work. Unfortunately, there was some lease-making that needed to take place, but we'd be able to sign first thing in the morning. I hung my head, kept my hope, and returned home. I recounted the experience of actually stepping foot into the apartment with Matt all night. It was too early to celebrate. After all, it had been taken back from us once before, but we banked on no official office business being done while all of the offices were closed. We could show up and have the lease signed before anyone would be able to process an appeal to stop us.

The next morning, we arrived about thirty minutes early to the lease signing appointment. We signed as soon as we were able, took the keys, and later days-ed out of the leasing office as soon as we could. As we beelined to the apartment building, I started to look around our new neighborhood, to take it all in. I took Matt up to the apartment, and there we were. It had finally happened. Our dream apartment was ours, and given the way rent stabilization laws work, we could stay as long as we wanted. We had been on so many adventures together, and this was the first time we had a good sense of security in our housing. We knew this was the place that we could build a home together. We could possibly raise our children here. The American midwestern dream of a home, that seemed impossible to us in New York City, was now a reality.

I had never lived in a nice new home that felt this stable. For a good chunk of my life, I lived in a mobile home with my parents and brother. Not that there's anything wrong with a mobile home, but you definitely don't forget that when you are handed an upgrade like this one. And you don't forget that feeling of maybe feeling less than. You don't forget the looks at school when people find out that you live in a mobile home, or that you don't even have your own room.

And I'm very proud to say we have kept our promise to use the apartment to serve people as much as we can. We've hosted many friends who need a safe haven in the middle of the city while running around. Friends who've needed a place to spend the holidays when they can't be with family. Many friends and family who want to visit the city but cannot afford the high cost of hotels have stayed on our pullout couch. We know we are not deserving of such an incredible blessing, and as much as we can share it, we will. The rollercoaster was worth it. The test was hard, but keeping hope is what got us through. A hope without any expectations. A hope not rooted in what you want to happen, but rather that whatever does happen will be what's best for you or for others. That is what we should cling to.

KEEP CONFIDENT

IN SCHOOL, I was an excellent student. Like, top-of-my-class-straight-A's GREAT in school. YES, this is me bragging, because when you know that you really nailed something, never let anyone dim your light. You carry that small insignificant success with you as if it were Prometheus' torch all the way to your grave! Now, while I made a great show like I loved school, it was all a complete and utter load of shit. It was probably my first foray into the "fake it until you make it" lifestyle that I still haven't stopped employing.

My parents threatened me to do well in school. And even though I dreaded going, or doing all the meaningless busy work, I had to at least act like I liked it. I had to pretend I liked it to get through it. To this day, as long as I tell myself that I just have to "fake it" for a few more hours to get through whatever crazy or incredible thing is happening at that moment, I can confidently push through.

It's like a thing you tell a toddler to get them out of their shell. Like, "Hey, you can do this thing, you are invisible, and no one can see you," and then boom, now they are fully eating a Happy Meal in public, and you are pleased with yourself for lying to a child. How do you feel now, child liar? Good about yourself? Well, you better! You just helped a child get over their agoraphobia in order to partake in nutrition that their body so desperately needs.

Much like a child learning to overcome their fears, we all need something that sparks us and drives us to face our fears head-on. Everyone is different, so one tactic might not work for you, even if it seems to work for everyone else. We have to do the digging until we can find what works for us and cling to it for as long as it works. In my opinion, this self-discovery needs to happen as early as possible in a person's life. But of course, this epiphany is usually delayed these days due to the recent rise of the helicopter parent.

I have peers who are unable to uncover their secrets well into their careers. It breaks my heart when I see them struggling, knowing the potential they have yet to unleash. Their parents did everything for them, so they weren't able to fail, hate things, or figure out what they were truly good at or enjoyed doing.

Even at the beginning of my life, people would always throw around the phrase, "Fake it 'til you make it," as the first option you should try when you attempt to do something you have never done before. But what they don't tell you is that you NEVER stop feeling like you are faking it! Ever. I heard that mantra, clung to it for dear life, and have never let go. Sometimes, it's the only thing that gets me through a challenge, whether it's my performance or taking a really hard test. I go in, making sure I feel as prepared as possible, when in actuality I probably am not. It's like a weird "mind over matter" type of thing that you read about monks doing. If I *feel* like I'm prepared, then maybe I actually am. I approached every scary audition or risky project with this mentality, and it has allowed me the freedom to dare to try every time.

Even now as I'm writing this book, I feel like a complete fraud that has no business writing a book. I feel like I am not funny, or even a good performer, but damn it if I'm not faking like I am! Because I have to. I fake it for anyone who might be helped by reading this, including someone like my younger self. That same younger self that would only make it through writing papers by making them about Broadway or video games.

As a matter of fact, English was the first class that I ever received a—*gasp*—B+. My teachers ripped my papers to shreds with their red pens. And while they may not have agreed with my "alternative grammar," I took pride in teaching them about a subject that *I* was interested in. (Shoutout to Professor Bilbro who had to read my papers on *Les Misérables* and *The Phantom of the Opera*.) But that hit to my writing confidence still persists. I just KNOW anyone who picks up this book will throw it in the trash after this chapter, write a bad review on Amazon, and comment something mean on my latest Instagram post.

And guess what? I don't really care, and this method still works for me! It somehow works brilliantly for me to preemptively accept that I might fail. I honestly think that this is some weird backward programming inside my brain, but hey, I'll take it! It's probably one of those things that conservatives would deem a mental illness in the forties, and I'd be ordered to be lobotomized. I mean hey, let's cure this and the gay all in one go, right?! HA! I say, HA! Alright, that may be an extreme analogy. I guess I'm more scarred by some conservative's reactions to an "other's" success than I thought.

But the beauty I've found in this method is that the acceptance of probable failure before I even begin a project is the very thing that gives me the confidence to try and oftentimes the confidence to excel. Think about it: if you've already come to terms with the fact that you will fail, which nine times out of ten you will, you have nothing to worry about. You already know the outcome. Much of what we fear is the unknown, so by replacing it with a known you are able to mitigate that fear. Even IF the known, in this case, is a less than desirable outcome. You know one hundred percent that you will fail, so you are already prepared for the onslaught of critics, the bad reviews, the deer-in-the-headlights look when people don't know what to say.

And yet, we must push on with the task at hand. Whether it's an obligation or a passion. Because that's life, isn't it? We can't just sit by and do nothing with all of this precious time. We should try to accomplish as much as we could possibly want but with zero expectations.

After the acceptance of a lot of failure, life just becomes a numbers game. I vehemently throw myself into crazy ambitious creative projects, anticipating that I will fail. Then when I don't? When I finally strike something that actually works, something I'm good at and brings joy or value to those who consume it? That is a win. That win is amplified ten thousand-fold and outshines the hundreds of failures that came before it. Again, if you fail nine times out of ten, you just have to wait for that tenth time.

You always hear the story of the actor almost giving up right before they get their big break. It's always the same, they had two cents in their bank account, they had just gone to apply as a floor hand mopper at the bus station for less than minimum wage, but they decided on a whim to go on one last audition before their first shift. Then boom! They got the role, two million dollars, and we got the entire library of work we have from Uzo Aduba. She had just given up on acting for good, then a few hours later, she received the call that she had booked *Orange is the New Black*.

Therein lies the problem. The majority of people do not stick it out. The majority of people get burnt out by attempt number three, or they let the bad comments about attempt number five scare them away from going for number six or seven. The majority of people stop just before the moment when they are most successful. I made a vow to myself when I was very young that I would not let that be me. I've been blessed to always be incredibly sure of myself. Confident, at least, that whatever I'm meant to do or be will come to pass.

My friends always ask how I'm able to push through messes time and time again and keep going. My nemesis thinks that it is some sort of entitled arrogance, but then again, he also told me that I likely wouldn't be successful in my career and should find something else to do with my life besides theatre. This dude was the one who was charged to cultivate my talent, as the chair of my college's theatre department. Instead of trying to teach me, he tried to extinguish me by refusing to see me in any role he originally saw a white person play.

He would later even try to convince me to give up my first professional acting job when I was cast in *Spring Awakening*. He could not fathom how a person could rehearse and perform in a show in another city, while also attending their college classes. Energized with unlimited spite, I did both, and even added a part-time job to the mix for added spice. Hopefully he can never again question the work ethic of a young adult, a Latino, or a gay man. As Queen Mariah Carey taught me: Success is the ultimate resistance.

Even when I fail trying something new, or when I fail at a higher level of something I'm good at, it is still an improvement. When you are born and raised fairly low in the hierarchy of the American dream, you can't really go much lower. So here I am, free from the hardest grasps of failure, able to put myself out there over and over again. This is what I wish most for everyone, especially since it is immensely fun! What would you do if you could try anything without worrying about what others thought?

Now, that doesn't mean that the setbacks, the nosedived projects, and the letdowns don't hurt. They do. They will. However, it does mean that I don't have the time to dwell on the pain of defeat for very long. Please remember, life is just a numbers game. Spend no more than a few hours in your sorrow. Give the failure a nice solid mourning, learn as much as you can about why you failed, then immediately start attempt number nine thousand!

One of my favorite things in the world of theatre is the post-mortem. After a project ends or a show closes, the entire production staff has what we call a post-mortem. This is a time when designers, directors, producers, etc. come together to discuss all the things about the project. Every department tries to pick out what worked incredibly well. These become the things they move into the "best practices" column and add to future productions. Then everyone discusses the things that went bad. It can be incredibly painful as a team to expose all of your mistakes that may not have been apparent to people in other departments.

I have specific memories of particularly painful post-mortems imprinted on my brain that I have carried with me into new projects. As humans, we often learn to avoid danger through pain. And in our new luxurious, comfortable lives, I think we forget how pain can be healthy for our future selves. When the pain is severe, we know we NEVER want to experience it again, so we avoid the same mistakes at all costs. So, those particular post-mortems needed to be painful, and boy were they.

Every part of the production is scrutinized. It is not dissimilar to how we sometimes treat ourselves. Maybe if we had budgeted for more time in the space before opening the show, we could've made the set ten times better. Maybe if we had a tight, enforceable contact with vendors, we wouldn't have had to go the cheap route with last-minute costume choices. It is the time when we all shed our old skin and grow into a better artist and theatre-maker.

Learning from these errors is the only way we grow. How we rethink the way we handle issues, streamline processes, and—most of all—how we foresee potential obstacles that can creep up and pull the rug out from under us in the future.

Coming to terms with our flaws is how we heal, especially if we acknowledge that many of the mistakes were our own fault and we knew better. We give the proper amount of grief and mourning to a project we loved but is gone. Then, after the post-mortem is done, the entire project is laid to rest, only remembered for what it was.

Through many post-mortems of shows and critiques of my own work, I've learned that I loved *learning*, not school. I actually quite hated the structures, rules, confinements, and all the red tape that comes with the American public education institution. I was frustrated that I had to learn only what the administration wanted me to learn instead of what I wanted. I was further miffed when I would finish my work and still had to spend my day chained to a desk, unable to actually be productive.

I love learning more than anything. Through constant learning, we continue to grow, and there is almost no limit to that growth. We can, of course, limit our own growth by refusing to acknowledge our weaknesses. Our arrogance can take hold when we believe that we know everything about a particular subject, and that is a dangerous place where growth is stunted. But learning more about a subject makes us better practitioners, and hopefully one day, experts!

And the best way to learn the most in one go is to have a big stinky turd of failure. When we fall flat on our face in front of a room full of important people, you better believe we will remember not to do that again, and do everything in our power to prevent us from doing it in the future. I know you've probably been told this before, but shut up, because we all need constant reminders. Why do we forget? Why, in the twenty-first century does society treat failure as some gross thing that only lame people do? Why are we still made to feel ashamed for something that is so natural and necessary for our growth? If you know, please send me the answer or resources to joshwadam@gmail.com.

So keep confident, knowing that you will fail most of the time. My life's motto is, "You win some, you lose most." This is how it is supposed to be. You will always fail, but as long as you keep analyzing what went wrong and get incrementally better each time, THAT is a success. That is your sign that you are on the right track to your next big win. Remember, it always goes step six, seven, eight, home run. Please don't let step five scare you from continuing. Don't let the rejection from number four keep you from attempting number five. Also, did I really just end this chapter with a sports reference? I'm so random sometimes!

KEEP CURIOUS

I GUESS YOU could say I've always had a thirst for adventure. After my brother's ordeal to become a real-life American hero, I had a strong sense of how lucky I was to have every single second of my life. Seconds are precious, limited, and the amount you're given is completely unknown to any of us on this Earth. My greatest fear is having regrets, so I set out to see, accomplish, and love as much as possible.

I don't necessarily think I've done a great job, but I definitely don't waste any more of my precious seconds beating myself up about it. Instead, I use that slight tinge of guilt about wasting time to fuel me into doing more, more, and more. The thrill of life for myself is how I can best myself on the next try. This book is hopefully a bit better than one of my Instagram captions. Will I have a next book? If so, it HAS to be more helpful, fun, and better written than this one.

It's that competition with myself that keeps me on my toes, excited for the work I want to do in the future. I'm excited for all of the ways I'll keep learning and growing into the person that I am meant to be. The thrill for me doesn't come from booking the next show or commercial. It comes from my love of running the race. And at the end of the day, I still get to build my family with my wonderful husband in our wonderful home, so I have no complaints.

We all have bucket list items we would hope to accomplish one day. Most of us sit around thinking about how cool it would be to actually check those things off of the list one day. Well, I'm here to tell you that that day is never going to come to you. It's up to you. You are the one that has to go out and make those experiences happen for yourself instead of waiting on the world to hand them to you. It's not that the world is against you, but maybe they just don't have the time.

But my rule for this kind of ambition is that you do not chase results! Chasing results will always make you compromise what you set out to do and will always leave you disappointed in the end. There will always be someone who traveled to more places than you, who got more followers than you, and who actually got a book published. Instead, I hope you chase the process. It's amazing you traveled to those places you wanted and got those few followers who engaged with the content *you* wanted to put out, not the content that you thought would do well. And it is absolutely amazing that you wrote the book you always meant to write.

In that spirit of curiosity of how much you can achieve, I also want to challenge you to keep curious about what your impact on your world can be. Somewhere along the way, probably through high school and early adult life, there are many forces telling us there is a limit on our impact. Whether that be because we don't have the funds, are too young or too inexperienced, or the thought that "our time will come." Every single one of us has the power to make a huge impact on those around us. A huge impact doesn't have to be an act that is noticed by a million people. Even if you bring a bit of hope, joy, and love to just one other person, that's a huge impact.

If everyone believed they could have a huge impact, the world would be brighter, more accepting, and more colorful. Positivity and gratitude are my mantras for life, and I don't care how cheesy or cliché that sounds to you right now. I'll continue to tell you that over and over again until you believe it. I have seen how a little positivity can drastically change lives. I have seen the power a little positivity can bring to someone just when they need it the most. And since we'll probably never know when someone needs it the most, how about we cover all of our bases and try to bring it to folks every day, in every action of our lives?

I, myself, will continue to stay curious about how I can find more opportunities to bring someone a healthy dose of love. I'll message people out of the blue with a thing I love about them, I'll schedule a coffee date or tea just to check-in and listen to them, or I'll send them a gift card to pay for their coffee that day. As I go along, I discover new ways to surprise people with things they love. Nothing feels as good as making someone smile. Giving back is healthy for us.

And in the spirit of being fair in my challenge, you've already given back to me. Thank you for reading my book! If you've made it this far, I'll give you credit for doing one positive thing for someone today, because you have indeed put a smile on my face.

When I set out to write this, I had no idea exactly what it was going to be. I knew I wanted to create something that I so desperately needed growing up, and most of all, I wanted to put a big dose of positive energy into the world in the very tumultuous time of a pandemic. One small gesture I could make to try and make the world a little better than how I found it.

While nothing in this book is perfect, while there may be some confusing sentences, or a comma out of place, I think I achieved just that. Again, it's not about being perfect, it's all about doing your best, and at least doing SOMETHING! I am beyond proud of myself for completing it. I hope kid Joshua would be proud, too.

If you have the time, I'd love to know what you think! You can do a lot to help me out, help me get better, and help us all continue to grow. You can leave a review of the book; you can share the book with a friend, share it on your own social media, or find me in-person and let me know what you think. This is the scariest project I've done to date. I know I'm good at telling other people's stories, but I'm not so sure about my own.

In the theatre, we can tell how our stories are being received by the audience in real time. If our timing is on, we get the roaring laugh that bellows throughout the space, halting the show and forcing us to hold on delivering our next line until it dies down. If we are present in our emotions, we can hear the sniffles and see the tears in the front row. While I'm used to getting an immediate audience response, without your help, I may never know how this book is received. It truly would make my day to hear from you in one way or another.

And with that, I'm on to the next adventure. Not quite sure what that will be just yet, but know that I'll give it my all. I'm no longer afraid of possible failure; it's outweighed by all the good things that can come of it. I'm fully prepared to step into the unfamiliar without any expectations. You'll never hit the home run if you don't swing the bat. (I don't even like baseball, why do I keep referencing it?) And now that we're friends, I hope to be at your next big adventure. If this little Texas boy can go on to have some pretty big adventures, so can you. If you feel like sharing, reach out to me on Instagram (@joshwadam) so I can cheer you on. You can do it!

And as always,
KEEP SWEET!
All my love,
Joshua

REVIEW KEEP SWEET

Write a review on your favorite book retailer's website and Goodreads!

This is the single best way to support authors and create awareness about books like *Keep Sweet*. Honest ratings and reviews mean the world to authors. If you loved the book, tell me what you loved. If you hated it, let me know! These reviews and ratings are an integral part of the book process and a great chance to listen to what our readers are saying about our work.

Your support is so deeply appreciated. I look forward to reading all of your reviews!

Besides reviews you can support independent authors by:

1. Buying and reading our books.
2. Requesting our books from your local libraries or independent book stores.
3. Gifting our books to loved ones.
4. Joining our communities on social media platforms.

ACKNOWLEDGMENTS

I'm forever grateful for those who read the first few pages, and then pushed me to complete this book journey, Edward, Bethany, Jenny, and Victoria. These writings started as a gratitude exercise during the 2020 pandemic. While the world was isolated, and the entertainment industry turned up side down, I was grateful to have a place to put all of my anxious energy. These folks saw the spark in those first unintelligible paragraphs, and helped transform them into one of the most rewarding projects I've ever worked on.

I also would love to thank Eric Myers of Myers Literary Management. He quickly became an ultimate champion for the queer, Latino story, and served as an incredible guide through the labyrinth of the publishing industry. I never would have believed that my book would be read by so many amazing editors at big publishing houses, and Eric made it happen over and over again. Even when I decided to self-publish this book, Eric maintained full, unconditional support and even helped me as much as possible. I can never thank you enough, Eric. Here's to the next one!

Where would I be without my favorite character in the book, my husband and my world, Matt. You continuously make me want to do better, be better, and try harder. You are the only one I want to impress. Thank you for always believing in every single crazy new project I decide to throw myself into. Thank you for all the nights of going to bed alone so I can write. Thank you for the resounding, "Yeah, it's good," after your first reading. Thank you for project-managing my entire life, let alone the creation of this book. I thank God everyday for the gift of you. I can't wait for the next project, our next adventure, and the next of my pitches you will have to operationalize.

Lastly, I'm forever grateful for you, dear reader. Thank you for reading words I wrote. Thank you for stepping into my world for a moment and living in the space of my life. I hope you had a great time, learned something about yourself, and truly know that you have a friend in me. Until next time.

ABOUT THE AUTHOR

Based in New York City, Joshua Gonzales is a Mexican-American performer and content creator best known for Guest Star and Co-Star roles on ABC, Lifetime, CNN, and theatre credits Off-Broadway, on National Tours, and on regional stages across America. For six years, Joshua served as a company member and communications associate for Third Rail Projects, the premier immersive theatre company based in New York City. Joshua holds a bachelor of fine arts degree in theatre performance. When not working, Joshua loves spending time with his husband making espresso martinis or hunting down the latest new pastry treat in the city. You can often find Joshua in the gym, blasting Mariah Carey through his earbuds.

Follow @joshwadam for all the latest!
Twitter | Instagram | TikTok